REFERENCE GUIDES IN LITERATURE

NUMBER 3

Joseph Katz, *General Editor*

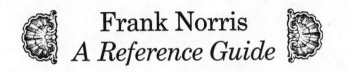

Frank Norris
A Reference Guide

Jesse S. Crisler
Joseph R. McElrath, Jr.

G. K. HALL & CO., 70 LINCOLN STREET, BOSTON, MASS. 1974

Library of Congress Cataloging in Publication Data

Crisler, Jesse S
   Frank Norris: a reference guide.

   (Reference guides in American literature, no. 3)
   1. Norris, Frank, 1870-1902--Bibliography.
I. McElrath, Joseph R., joint author. II. Title.
Z8633.C75   016.813'4   74-14956
ISBN 0-8161-1097-2

This publication is printed on permanent/durable acid-free paper.

Contents

Introduction

The word "definitive" is popular today. One hears of "definitive" editions, "definitive" biographies, and even of "definitive"
critical studies. From a limited viewpoint such works may indeed
seem to be definitive--until six months or six years later, when
someone else produces a still more "definitive" piece of scholarship.
That kind of escalated "definitiveness" takes place so regularly that
William B. Dillingham (1971.5) ran a considerable risk when he termed
Kenneth A. Lohf and Eugene P. Sheehy's Frank Norris: A Bibliography
(1959.7) the definitive bibliography. Neither Lohf nor Sheehy made
that claim; and, as it happens, Dillingham was wrong. There is no
definitive bibliography of Frank Norris, nor will one ever exist.
All that is possible is for scholars to add, incrementally, information to that gathered by their predecessors, and to reassess contin-
ually the situation in the light of that new information. That is
what we have tried to do in Frank Norris: A Reference Guide for
writings about Norris.

We have built on the work of our predecessors in this area;
Lohf and Sheehy (1959.7), Joseph Gaer (1934.4), William White (1959.
12), and John S. Hill (1970.5).[1] To their considerable work we have
added what we found while surveying for the Centenary Edition of the
Works of Frank Norris the magazines, newspapers, and books in
Norris's time, and scholarly journals and books published through
the end of 1972. (We have included material published in 1973, but
for then we are even less likely to claim "definitiveness" than for
the earlier years: we included what we found, but we know that we
have not found everything--not even everything important). The
result, we believe, is a fuller body of data which should enable
serious students to have not only a broader view of Norris's life
and work than was possible before, but also several new vantage
points from which to approach the problems of Norris biography,
bibliography, and criticism.

---

[1] We are also indebted to bibliographical data in 1942.4, 1962.3,
1967.1, 1969.3, and 1971.5, as well as in Clayton L. Eichelberger, A Guide to
Critical Reviews of United States Fiction, 1870 - 1910 (Metuchen: The Scarecrow
Press, 1971).

INTRODUCTION

Entries are arranged chronologically, by year of publication, and thereafter alphabetically by author. Such an arrangement immediately reveals patterns important to any scholar: because the quantitative response to an author is a valid index to his reception and reputation, the chronological arrangement becomes a kind of rough graph indicating the ebb and flow of interest in his work. For Norris that graph confirms some already-known facts: that his status as a writer declined within a few years after his death, and that only since the end of World War II has his work been given the renewed attention afforded major--or minor-major--American writers. Each entry is numbered. These numbers are used in the "Author Index," where all of the authors we have been able to identify are listed alphabetically, and "Selected Subject and Title Index" at the back of this volume. Thus, in either index, a reference to 1903.21 directs the user to entry 21 in year 1903. A dagger (†) following an entry number in the "Selected Subject and Title Index" identifies the item as a review of the work cited. When the work cited in the "Selected Subject and Title Index" is a shorter one, the entry refers to a larger work in which it is included. For example "After Strange Gods," 1928.12, is published in The Argonaut Manuscript Limited Edition of Frank Norris' Works, X, which is the entry citation.

The "Selected Subject and Title Index" alphabetically lists categories for bibliographical information ("Bibliography") and biographical data ("Biography"), as well as for each of Norris's works that has received any significant attention. That last category raises the inevitable question of objectivity. Of course we have our own opinions about the value of individual writings about Norris, but we have seen our function in this Reference Guide as one that requires as much objectivity as we could master. But objectivity is not the same as automatism; it involves the exercise of judgment towards the goal of fairness. Unfortunately, judgment can easily slide into realms that defeat the need for objectivity. All this sounds like circular reasoning, but it is not. It is preliminary to a note on our application of the term "significant" to the construction of the "Selected Subject and Title Index." An article which deals exclusively with one work is of course considered "significant" comment on that work (whatever our private opinions of its merit) and therefore is indexed under the work's title. More often, however, the writing touches on more than one work, and it is in such cases that we have exercised our judgment about whether or not to index. For instance, the mere mention of Moran of the Lady Letty in scholarship published in 1968 is judged insignificant, and so no reference to that scholarly work appears under the title of that novel in the "Subject Index." But even a brief reference to Moran of the Lady Letty as an interesting earlier novel by Norris in a 1900 review of A Man's Woman is considered of considerable importance to the student of Norris's place in the turn-of-the-century literary world, and that reference is included in the index.

We have seen, in one form or another, everything listed here.
And, except for doctoral dissertations and works in foreign languages,
which are listed in sections separate from the main section, we have
annotated all entries.[2] Our annotations developed from the same
concerns that informed the "Subject Index": we have attempted to
supply brief abstracts of the writings, noting as best we could their
main theses or topics, and emphasizing as well as we were able their
most consequential points.

I

The major statement on Norris's contemporary reputation is Paul
H. Bixler's "Frank Norris's Literary Reputation" (1934.1).[3] Although
Bixler is more specific about sources of his information than Franklin D. Walker was in Frank Norris: A Biography (1932.10), he pictures Norris's situation during his own time in almost exactly the
way Walker did. The resonance of anticipation and confirmation that
Bixler created in that fashion has been the dominant theme in that
area of Norris studies ever since. But Bixler presented serious dis-
tortions that must be corrected. For example, consider the following
two remarks which Bixler used as brush strokes to broadly paint
Norris into his own time, and therefore in American literary history:

> His [early] reception, in spite of his sponsor's [i.e.,
> Howell's] aid, was cold. ...with his third attack
> [i.e., The Octopus], the adamantine walls of clois-
> tered criticism [i.e., the genteel critics] were bat-
> tered off their foundations. [P. 109.]

Little about either of those statements has any basis in verifiable
reality. Regarding the second, we have found absolutely no evidence
that Norris—with either The Octopus or The Pit—fit the battle or
won the Realistic war that Howells formally initiated. Certainly,
reviews of those two novels do nothing to indicate that Norris's
contemporaries—genteel or not—felt that way about them, nor do
posthumous evaluations by the novelists and critics who wrote soon
after Norris died. Bixler seems to have been telling a good story,
but only a story. Regarding the first statement, the newly-enlarged
body of reviews on Moran of the Lady Letty, McTeague, and Blix—the
first three novels published by Norris—contradicts the notion of a
"cold" reception. Certainly, there was no deluge from reviewers
about Moran of the Lady Letty: it was a first novel by an unknown.
But there was a respectable number of reviews; and while those by
Americans were not overwhelmingly positive, many of them were favorable. In England, where Moran of the Lady Letty was published as

---

[2] We have divided responsibility for writings in English. The entries
for 1891 - 1920 are primarily the work of McElrath. Crisler is primarily
responsible for 1921 - 1973.

[3] Page numbers in parentheses throughout the text of this introduction
refer to Bixler's article (1934.1).

Shanghaied in 1899, the reviews were extremely favorable. And many
reviewers on both sides of the Atlantic found Blix more than just
"an hour's excellent entertainment." George Hamlin Fitch of the
San Francisco Chronicle, in fact, rated it the height of literary
art (1899.23). Even if his praise is set down as the homage of one
home-town boy to another, many other reviewers stand next to him in
judging Blix enjoyable and worthwhile.

　　　Let us turn from Bixler for a moment to remark an aspect of the
Blix reviews that no one has yet considered. Norris had followed the
adventure romance of Moran of the Lady Letty with the boldly naturalistic McTeague; then, in Blix, he moved in still a third direction,
completely unanticipated by the first two. Aside from the merits of
Blix itself, many reviewers enthusiastically noted that here was the
work of an American novelist whose talents were various. In 1901
The Octopus would jolt the literary world into seeing Norris as a
contender for achieving "The Great American Novel" (a recognition
Howells had made in 1899, after reading Moran of the Lady Letty and
McTeague). But in 1899, with three early novels behind him, Norris
was already creating a sensation of sorts. Reviewers were discover-
ing a multi-faceted talent from whom, as many said, they expected
great things to come. Now, back to Bixler: he completely missed
this important phase of Norris's reception; probably for want of
sufficient data, he termed it "cold", and thereby created the distorted impression that is dominant today.

　　　Bixler also distorts, in another way, Howells's regard for
Moran of the Lady Letty and McTeague, and this distortion is perhaps
more serious in its implications than the other. It is as if he
formulated his thesis that Howells had little regard for those two
novels, then chose selectively Howells's expressions of reserve to
support his thesis. He cites Howells's admission of excitement in
reading Moran of the Lady Letty, then jumps to his critical dis-
claimer, "I do not consider my own gasps criticism" (P. 110). On
McTeague, Bixler quotes only Howells's comment that it is "a remarkable book"--then immediately cites weaknesses found by Howells in it
(P. 111). In this way, Bixler buries the important by stressing its
natural qualifications, thus distorting Howells's extremely favorable
response to Norris. The points Howells made were preponderantly
positive: that Norris seemed to signal the emergence of a continental American fiction insofar as he worked with native American
materials in an American way; that in Moran of the Lady Letty he
had cast his story "in the light of common day"; and that in Mc-
Teague Norris effectively captured and conveyed the atmosphere of
his subject in a remarkably realistic manner. And there were other
reviewers who agreed with Howells. So while Norris's early work
did not sell as well as The Octopus or The Pit, he was not the
near-loser that Bixler implies. Our researches have revealed that
the Norris of Moran of the Lady Letty, McTeague and Blix was viewed
quite differently from the hack-writer that his later critics have
seen. There is nothing to prevent them from continuing to see him

that way, of course, but right reason should prevent them from
calling for the non-existent support of his early reviewers--at
least, on those of them whom we have found.

New data on the critical reception of A Man's Woman also should
correct the present image of that novel's significance to Norris's
career. Today it is virtually a universally disliked book. But it
was the best-selling work of Norris's career through 1900. Bixler's
1934 criticism of the work is mild compared to the negative reaction
expressed after World War II: he tamely declares that "It is never
quite real" (P. 114), explaining its popularity as possibly resulting
from "the widespread interest in arctic exploration at the turn of
the century." That is indeed probable. But what is certain is the
fact that Norris created a violent sensation with what most reviewers
considered a shockingly brutal and sometimes sickening book. Reviewers of Blix had explained Norris's turn from the hard realism of
McTeague to a sunshine-filled love idyll as a sign that he had
learned his lesson regarding what the reading public wanted. In A
Man's Woman, however, Norris turned from the ideal and, to the reviewer's minds, out-did McTeague in offensiveness. A graphic account
of Arctic suffering, a minute description of surgery, and even the
braining of a horse with a hammer--the response to all this was out-
rage greater than that which had greeted McTeague. Literary historians repeatedly point to McTeague as a book which dramatically paved
the way for more radical departure from the accepted and expected,
but A Man's Woman merits equal attention in this regard. The new
reviews presented here indicate clearly why Norris was told to revise
his novel for its second printing.

Bixler's commentary on the response to The Octopus, The Pit, and
the posthumously-published collections of short stories and essays is
sound. Reviewers would occasionally chide Norris for stylistic
faults of repetitiveness and overexuberance, but those two novels
were accorded almost universal respect. Some found fault with The
Octopus's apparently contradictory conclusion, though most did not;
and formal debate over its inconsistencies did not begin in earnest
until the 1940s. With The Pit, reviewers did, as Bixler says, fall
"over themselves in praise" (P. 117). To most reviewers, Norris
had at last gotten his style and structure under control and had
produced a relatively finished work of art--though there were a
few reviewers who saw it differently as do most critics today.

As for the posthumously-published collections of short stories--
A Deal in Wheat and The Third Circle--they were, and are now, held in
relatively low regard, containing only moments of greatness and mainly simple indications of the fictional tendencies that Norris would
follow and perfect in his novels. The essays in The Responsibilities
of the Novelist were interesting, and, to some, stimulating, but they
were valuable mainly because they revealed something of the attitudes
of Norris the novelist. When Vandover and the Brute appeared in
1914, the reaction was in the main nebulous, apparently because
Charles G. Norris and his promotional pamphlet (1914.12) for Vandover

provided the script that most of the reviews followed, rehearsing
the story of a miraculous discovery of the manuscript, Charles's
insistence that the novel was unfinished, and his view that the
novel was a bit of apprentice work. Some reviewers innovated upon
that script by insisting that it was still a remarkable study of an
individual's degeneration; others were politely shocked; and one
suggested that it should have been bowlderized. But, compared to
the reviews during Norris's lifetime, the response was dull. Between 1898 and 1903 Norris was clearly a physical presence and there
was a vital tension to be observed between him and the literary
world. By 1914 this tension had gone slack--despite the sometimes
excited and effusive introductions written for the Argonaut Manuscript Limited Edition of Frank Norris's Works in 1928--and it has
largely remained thus up to the present. Bixler's attitude towards
Norris and his conception of Norris's place in his own time are to a
large degree the prevalent ones now. The one exception in Norris
studies is to be seen in the lively wrangling that continues over
what exactly were Norris's intentions in The Octopus.

II

William B. Dillingham, in the "Frank Norris" chapter of Fifteen
American Authors Before 1900 (1971.5) gives a sound, detailed description of the flurry of critical controversy involving The Octopus.
Indeed, he gives such a complete picture of critical trends in Norris
studies from the time of Norris's death through the 1960s that the
data we indicate in our entries requires little commentary. For the
most part, our new entries complement the picture Dillingham has
drawn, rather than alter it. Except for one critical trend in the
1930s--when Granville Hicks and others applied the term of "muck-
raker" to Norris for his performance in The Octopus--the main thrusts
of Norris criticism have become relatively consistent. The first is
that Norris was a literary naturalist, though of course not a "pure"
example of the breed. Major book-length statements such as Franklin
Walker's Frank Norris: A Biography (1932.10), Ernest Marchand's Frank
Norris: A Study (1942.4), and William B. Dillingham's Frank Norris:
Instinct and Art (1969.3) support this notion.[4] W. M. Frohock's
pamphlet, Frank Norris (1969.5) says very little about Norris except
that he was the American disciple of Emile Zola. The second thrust
holds that Norris is more properly termed a romantic, a thesis re-
ceiving its first full-scale elaboration in Charles C. Walcutt's
American Literary Naturalism: A Divided Stream (1956.4), and given
greater exposition in Warren French's Frank Norris (1962.3), as
French stressed the notion that Norris was a scion of the American
transcendentalists. The third, and now most influential thurst, is
that recently initiated by Donald Pizer in The Novels of Frank Norris

_____
[4] In 1969.3, Dillingham attempts to discard labels and to approach Norris
primarily as a writer; and in 1971.5 laments the fact that many critics and
historians have wrongly presumed that they comprehended Norris with the term
"naturalist." However, the effect of Dillingham's own work is to reinforce
the belief that Norris is a naturalist.

(1966.3) and the series of articles that anticipated the points made
in that study. The main point made is that Norris in his novels was
a philosophically-consistent Le Contean evolutionary idealist--and
most scholars seem to have accepted it. At least, the dissertations
finished after the publication of Pizer's study indicate that his
views have gained a following and are likely to prove the major in-
forming influence on Norris criticism and biography for some time to
come. The fourth thrust, if it can be termed that, is a general
lack of respect, and sometimes apparent dislike, for the quality of
Norris's thought and expression. French hardly ever passes by an
opportunity to laugh at what he considers Norris's melodramatic
absurdities and stylistic idiosyncracies, and at one point he ques-
tions Norris's mental health. Using Zola as a standard for judgment,
Frohock frequently speaks of Norris in a tone of sophisticated be-
musement. Dillingham writes of Norris's chilling condescension towards his characters in McTeague and laments his racism. Virtually
all critics of the 1950s and 1960s pause to point out Norris's clumsi-
ness and inability to control his excesses. Ultimately, one comes
to wonder why, exactly, so many people--though admittedly the number
is not vast--spend so much time writing about a novelist who seems to
give them so little pleasure. As a naturalist, or romantic, or phil-
osopher-novelist, or just plain writer, Norris rarely seems to make
it past the evaluation tags of "amusing", "mediocre", "confused",
or "interesting;" and it sometimes seems that if Norris were not
"historically important" few commentators would have bothered to
comment at all.

Either Norris is inadequate or the various pigeonholes into
which critics and historians have placed him are. Perhaps the problem lies in both. But, then again, the experiment of coming to grips
with a writer who was considered unique in his own time and who might
still merit the description is only seventy years old, and it strikes
us that not many students of Norris and his time have devoted themselves to a thorough, continuing consideration of his work. Someone
new to Norris studies will find an image of stasis. It may appear
that all of the problems have been resolved in a "definitive" way.
But the illusion should soon pass. As the expanded list of reviews
in this Reference Guide indicates, few of the problems are anywhere
near being solved. We are only now gathering the primary data from
which we can truly assess Norris's place in the literary world of
the 1890s and 1900s, and we expect to find a good deal more in the
years ahead. Add to this the fact that very little biographical
work on Norris has been done since Walker's 1932 Frank Norris:
A Biography--the only biography. Consider then that we do not even
have sound texts of his novels, short stories, essays, and poems:
we do not know exactly what Norris wrote. Finally, note that we
still have not arrived at a complete list of all the pieces of which
Norris was the author. Only recently, in the 1973 volume of Proof
(1973.4), has Joseph Katz provided an attempt at a complete, resolved
bibliography of Norris's shorter writings, adding many new titles;
and he tells us that still more new items have turned up since its
publication.

INTRODUCTION

Norris studies, perhaps, may be only now making real beginnings. For, looking back from 1974, it is difficult to review the
present body of writing about Frank Norris and believe that it represents anything approaching finality, "definitive" as it may seem
to some. Surely the best is to come.

JESSE S. CRISLER

JOSEPH R. MC ELRATH, JR.

Acknowledgments

This bibliographical reference guide is indebted to a good many people. Among them are Joseph Katz, who first suggested to us the need for such a guide in 1971, and generously made available to us his collection of writings concerning Norris. James D. Hart allowed us to make free use of The Frank Norris Collection at The Bancroft Library of The University of California, Berkeley. Beverly Brooks of the McKissick Library, University of South Carolina, diligently labored for two years to acquire materials we needed to examine through interlibrary loan. Indeed, all of the staff of the McKissick Library was very helpful. Brent L. Kendrick of the <u>Proof</u> Editorial Office repeatedly took time from his own work to inform us of relevant data he had run across; Mark A. Anderson generously surrendered time from his own work at the British Museum to make checks for us in British newspapers and magazines.

PUBLISHED WRITINGS IN ENGLISH ABOUT FRANK NORRIS

1891

1   "Book News of the Week," New York Herald (December 13), p. 26.
         In smooth and flowing rhyme and rhythm Norris presents
     one of the best narrative poems to appear in a long time.
     With excellent color plates and the best of paper and bind-
     ing, Yvernelle is a "holiday book of the better kind."

2   "New Publications," Lippincott's Magazine, XLVIII (December),
     647-48.
         Yvernelle is a "free and flowing fancy of the days of
     knight-errantry." The character of Sir Caverlaye, his fight
     with the brother of Guhaldrada, and his night ride to the
     church are the most admirable features of the poem. The
     physical make-up of the book is splendid.

3   ORACLE, K. B. "A Letter About Books," The Wave, VII (December
     26), 9.
         Yvernelle is "an exceedingly clever piece of work," es-
     pecially for someone who is still a college student. Sev-
     eral passages contain "descriptive writing that show[s]
     touches of real poetic fire and fancy." The illustrations
     are the "finest...seen this season."

4   "Weekly Record of New Publications," Publishers' Weekly, XL
     (December 12), 987.
         Briefly summarizes Yvernelle. The reviewer finds that
     it "tells a moving tale," but is more impressed by the
     book's design. He praises the excellent color reproductions
     and decorative details.

5   "'Yvernelle,'" The Critic, XIX (December 5), 316.
         Yvernelle is a well sustained, interesting poem with
     "plenty of swing and music." Norris knows "how to tell a
     story and also how to write in the manner of Sir Walter."
     The illustrations are especially good.

1891

6   "Yvernelle," <u>Publishers' Weekly</u> ("Christmas Bookshelf" issue), XL (November 21-28), 36.
        <u>Yvernelle</u> is a skillfully worded and stirring poem that makes some very telling points when Norris compares "the feudal baron of yore with the money-kings of today." The reviewer describes and praises the book's design.

1892

1   "The Books of 1891: Art Books," <u>Publishers' Weekly</u>, XLI (January 30), 204.
        <u>Yvernelle</u> is mentioned as one of the noteworthy illustrated books of 1891.

2   "Recent Poetry," <u>The Nation</u>, LIV (March 31), 254.
        Brief reference to <u>Yvernelle</u> as an "obvious" example of the "highly wrought romance of chivalry." It is a book "whose wealth of costly illustrations only makes the verse seem tamer."

3   "Yvernelle," <u>Overland Monthly</u>, XIX (January), 106.
        <u>Yvernelle</u> is interesting, "sparkles here and there with an apt and pretty figure," and rises to "a good deal of dramatic force in the fight of Canto II and in Sir Caverlaye's ride. The book is a "marvel of printer's art."

1893

1   MIGHELS, ELLA S. C. "California Writers and Literature," <u>The Story of the Files</u>. San Francisco: Co-operative Printing Company, pp. 359-60.
        <u>Yvernelle</u> is a "strong performance," containing many passages of fine descriptive writing and several episodes of marked dramatic force.

1897

1   DAVENPORT, ELEANOR M. "Frank Norris," <u>The University of California Magazine</u>, III (November), 80-82.
        Recounts Norris's life to 1897. Norris is a very talented illustrator who, upon his return from study in Paris, turned his attentions to literature. He possesses a good deal of insight into human nature, and his writings for <u>The Wave</u> have greatly helped to raise its quality. Norris has recently transcended the influences of Richard Harding

1898

Davis and Rudyard Kipling to develop a style of his own:
"Vivid, graphic description is his strong point." His
collection of short stories, entitled "Ways That Are Dark,"
is "now in press."

1898

1   BONNER, GERALDINE. "A Californian's Novel, "Argonaut, XLIII
      (November 21), 7.
         Norris's short stories have always attempted to "give
      reality to the unusual." But they have never been convinc-
      ing because of a lack of effective imaginative force. In
      Moran of the Lady Letty Norris has "at last got real control
      of his story"--at least for the first half, which moves for-
      ward "with strength, firmness, and an exultant force and
      sincerity." With the introduction of Moran he lost control
      and the story became a "series of adventures, more or less
      episodical and unnatural." Norris apparently became con-
      scious of the "falseness of the work" and grew tired of it.

2   "Briefer Notices," Public Opinion, XXV (October 13), 473.
         Sarcastic summary of Moran of the Lady Letty. The re-
      viewer concludes that Ross's loss of Moran "was probably a
      piece of good fortune for both." He rates the story as
      "readable, but not above the average."

3   HOWELLS, WILLIAM DEAN. "American Letter", Literature, III
      (December 17), 577-78.
         If the reader will grant Norris his working hypothesis,
      he will find Moran of the Lady Letty "a clever little story"
      whose incidents "follow one another with a profusion and
      rapidity which leave one little leisure for question of
      their probability." The hero is realistically drawn, and
      the story "gains a certain effectiveness from being so
      boldly circumstanced in the light of common day, and in a
      time and place of our own." Whoever wishes a thrill will
      find it in Moran.

4   J. K. W. "Along Literary Pathways," New Orleans Times-Democrat
      (December 18), p. 26.
         Refers to "Miracle Joyeux" in McClure's Magazine as "a
      charming sketch...by...an author who has succeeded admirably
      with a theme not easy to handle."

1898

5   [MARCOSSON, ISAAC F.] "A Splendid Story of the Sea", Louisville
    Times (November 26), p. 7.
        Moran of the Lady Letty is "one of the best sea tales of
    the year." The analysis of Moran's "heart" is strong but
    "intensely human" and told in a brilliantly "clever" style.

6   "'Moran of the Lady Letty'", Buffalo Morning Express (November
    20), p. 18.
        "The story is steep in places, but it has the taste of
    the sea in it." Moran of the Lady Letty "enthralls the
    reader."

7   "Moran of the Lady Letty", Literary World, XXXIX (November 26),
    404.
        The reviewer finds Moran of the Lady Letty "a very queer
    story" and summarizes it in a sarcastic tone. He is re-
    lieved that Moran was knifed and did not have to live in
    society with Ross: "To imagine her civilizing into a fe-
    male gilded youth, with a knowledge of dress, deportment,
    salted almonds, and tea-table chatter, is too great a stretch
    of human fancy."

8   "Novels and Tales," The Outlook, LX (October 8), 394-95.
        Moran of the Lady Letty is "a dramatic story of the sea."

9   "Recent Fiction", Washington Times (October 30), p. 20.
        The characterization of Moran and the daring conception
    of casting a civilized man into prehistorical conditions
    make Moran of the Lady Letty "one of the best sea novels
    of the year." It is "vivid, strong, forceful," and the
    "man who can write such a tale...should be able to do other
    good work of an unusual sort."

10 "Weekly Record of New Publications," Publishers' Weekly, LIV
    (October 1), 520.
        The reviewer terms the story of Moran of the Lady Letty
    "exciting." He notes the "graphic" description of the
    Lady Letty's sinking and cites Moran as, "aside from Wilbur,
    the most interesting personage in the singular novel."

                        1899

1   [ABBOTT, EDWARD, AND MADELINE VAUGHN.] "McTeague," Literary
    World, XXX (April 1), 99.
        A rejoinder to Barry (1899.6). Norris is unquestionably
    a powerful and skillful writer, but great art is not merely
    a matter of execution. McTeague is a "remarkable" book, but

not a great one because of Norris's unnecessary "sins against good taste and delicacy." Norris's presentation of "grossness for the sake of grossness is unpardonable."

2   "American Fiction", Athenaeum (December 2), 757.
        The reviewer notes the peculiarities of California speech presented in McTeague. After briefly summarizing the story, he concludes: "No personage in this melodramatic tale is pleasing, yet the story is vigorously told and readable."

3   "Among The New Books," Chicago Daily Tribune, LVIII (February 2), 8.
        Moran of the Lady Letty is a very "uncommon" tale of adventure, especially in its depiction of the violent manner in which the hero wins the heroine's love. "The style of the story is always lively."

4   [BANGS, JOHN KENDRICK.] "The Compleat Novelist," Literature, V (November 17), 449-50.
        Whereas Blix's hero, Condy, goes directly "to nature for both essentials and details" in his writings, and thus proves himself a "true realist," Norris borrows from other writers. Captain Jack's story of buried whiskey came from a New York City Sunday paper. The joke of Kitty's encyclo-pedic education is very old. And the telegram ploy was borrowed from Arthur Conan Doyle. (See Stronks [1970.14] for a discussion of this review.)

5   BANKS, NANCY HUSTON. "Two Recent Revivals In Realism," The Bookman (American), IX (June), 356-57.
        After praising the recent trend in novelistic fiction toward "works of ideality and romance," Banks laments Norris's "hard and cold" manner as he touches upon the "untouchable" in McTeague. Yet, she admits that McTeague is "absolutely interesting." It "seizes and holds in a vise-like grip that is almost painful from the beginning to the end of the story."

6   BARRY, JOHN D. "New York Letter," Literary World, XXX (March 18), 88-89.
        While too often we see Norris "pulling the strings" of his characters in McTeague, it ranks "among the few great novels" produced in America. With a profound insight into character, shrewd humor, a brilliant use of significant detail, and a fearless handling of subject matter, Norris makes a vivid presentation of the comic and pathetic in life. (See Abbott [1899.1] for a rejoinder.)

1899

7   BEACH, E. D. "New and Entertaining Fiction," The Book Buyer,
     XVIII (April), 244.
         Although it seems that Beach did not read much past the
     first chapter, he declares McTeague to be "vigorously told":
     "here is realism."

8   "Blix", Baltimore Sun (October 2), p. 10.
         In contrast with McTeague, Blix tells a "happy and pleas-
     ant story."

9   "Blix", Detroit Free Press (October 2), p. 7.
         Blix is quite different from Moran of the Lady Letty and
     the "repellant" McTeague. Yet, this "charming little love
     idyll" merits the same praise Howells bestowed upon McTeague:
     it abounds in little miracles of observation and moments of
     vivid insight. A "crisp," "spicy," and "humorous" book,
     Blix successfully presents a "leaf from the drama of common-
     place life" with "delicious" realism.

10   "Blix", The Outlook, LXIII (October 14), 419.
         Blix is a "refreshing contrast" to the "powerful and
     disagreeable" McTeague. It is "slight" and has its "improb-
     abilities and crudities," but is also "light-hearted" and
     "jolly."

11   "Blix", Overland Monthly, XXXIV (November), 474-75.
         Blix is "vastly interesting," but it will disappoint
     those who have expected something "big" from Norris. While
     Norris again exhibits his "remarkable descriptive powers"
     and draws a "first-rate" heroine, Blix is carelessly con-
     structed and marred by the "bad English" Norris assigns
     to the characters. Norris can do better work.

12   "Briefer Notices," Public Opinion, XXVI (March 16), 347.
         The reviewer regrets that Norris, after writing the
     "original" and "well-constructed" Moran of the Lady Letty,
     has turned his attention to the "degraded side of humanity"
     in McTeague. "It is a good story, but we trust that Mr.
     Norris's next plot will fall in more pleasant places."

13   "Briefer Notices," Public Opinion, XXVII (October 26), 538.
         Blix is an attractive book because of its simplicity and
     unassuming frankness.

14   "A California Novelist," Washington Times (October 15), pt. 2,
     p. 8.
         After the "tentative" adventure story of Moran of the
     Lady Letty, McTeague settled Norris's right to a place in

American literature. These first two books were very dif-
ferent from each other, and Blix represents yet another direction in which Norris has chosen to move. In some re-
spects Blix is his finest work. A man with such skill and
versatility may--as we hoped Harold Frederic would--write
the "great American novel."

15   [CATHER, WILLA.] "Books and Magazines," Pittsburgh Leader
       (March 31), p. 8.
          In this enthusiastic review of McTeague, Cather notes
       that, without signs of imitation, Norris has used the
       methods of Zola to great effect. The description of Polk
       Street especially demonstrates Norris's power, imagination,
       and literary skill. Norris effectively creates the illusion
       of life with a touch that is "heavy and warm and human."

16   [CATHER, WILLA.] "Books and Magazines," Pittsburgh Leader
       (November 4), p. 5.
          After the remarkably insightful but disagreeable and
       charmless McTeague, Norris has now given us an idyll, Blix,
       "that sings through one's brain like summer wind and makes
       one feel young enough to commit all manner of indiscre-
       tions." In turning from McTeague and the school of Zola,
       Norris has exhibited remarkable versatility.

17   [CATHER, WILLA.] "Books and Magazines," Pittsburgh Leader
       (November 11), p. 9.
          Cather begins her review of Stephen Crane's Active
       Service, thus, "After reading such a delightful newspaper
       story as....'Blix,' it is with assorted sensations of pain
       and discomfort that one closes the covers of another news-
       paper novel, 'Active Service.'"

18   CHAMBERLIN, JOSEPH EDGAR. "With a Paper-cutter," Boston Evening
       Transcript (November 22), p. 12.
          Blix seems to be the result of the reproaches Norris
       received for the gloomy and brutal McTeague. Norris has
       now written a "jolly" story that contains some fine touches
       --though Blix does occasionally border on the "trashy."
       Blix is inferior to McTeague: ironically, the "beautiful
       story of the love of old Grannis and Miss Baker" imbedded
       in McTeague is a much better piece of work than this book-
       length attempt at a love idyll.

1899

19   "The Christmas Bookstalls," <u>Boston Evening Transcript</u> (December
        6), p. 14.
                <u>Blix</u> is listed as one of "the more important works of
        fiction" of the year. The reviewer briefly summarizes the
        plot and then charges Norris with having plagiarized from
        Oliver Wendell Holmes's <u>The Autocrat of the Breakfast Table</u>.

20   COOPER, FREDERIC TABER. "Frank Norris, Realist", <u>The Bookman</u>
        (American), X (November), 234-38.
                Norris's literary creed is realism, and yet, paradox-
        ically, "he has an obstinate and often exasperating vein of
        romanticism running through all his work." Norris's true
        greatness is in his "gift of depicting the physical side of
        life," especially on a grand scale.

21   D.   "Blix", <u>Pacific Monthly</u>, VIII (December), 82.
                In marked contrast to <u>McTeague</u>, <u>Blix</u> is a hopeful book
        in which ethical purpose is predominant. It is not so
        exciting as <u>McTeague</u>, but the characters are well drawn, as
        are Norris's descriptions of San Francisco and the natural
        landscape surrounding it.

22   "Fiction", <u>Dundee Advertiser</u> (March 20), p. 2.
                <u>Shanghaied</u> must be rated very highly as a "refreshingly
        original and clever" adventure story. The action is "brisk
        and surprising," and the scenes are "extremely picturesque
        and riotously redolent of the sea." Moran is a character
        "whose like has not before appeared in fiction." It should
        become popular.

23   FITCH, GEORGE HAMLIN. "Among The New Books," <u>San Francisco
        Chronicle</u> (October 8), p. 4.
                In contrast with the "hard realism" of <u>McTeague</u> and the
        "wild adventure" of <u>Moran of the Lady Letty</u>, <u>Blix</u> is "a
        very delightful love idyll" which contains more and better
        local color writing than any other novel in print. The
        characters are very realistically drawn. The only jarring
        element is Norris's preoccupation with Blix's odors. Other-
        wise, her portrait, as many of the scenes, is "wonderfully
        well done." "This is the height of literary art."

24   [GILDER, JEANETTE.] "The Lounger," <u>The Critic</u>, XXXIV (May),
        398.
                Dubbing Norris "the American Balzac," Gilder praises the
        "strange and impressive story" of <u>McTeague</u>. She could not
        put down this "horribly realistic, but...never coarse"
        novel.

25 "A Good Story," The New Age (London), XIX (March 30), 155.
Shanghaied is a "remarkably well-written piece of work"
with "unflagging interest." Wilbur's reappearance in polite
society is especially good. Kitchell is "uncommonly good
company, especially when sober." It is a pity that he dies
so soon. There is a "vigorous, descriptive power, a bright-
ness, and withal a humour displayed...that likes us well."

26 HOWELLS, WILLIAM DEAN. "A Case in Point," Literature, n. s.
No. 1 (March 24), pp. 241-42.
When reading Moran of the Lady Letty Howells suspected it
a sign of an emerging "continental American fiction," and
McTeague has confirmed his expectations of Norris. In this
"remarkable" book, strongly reminiscent of Zola's "epical
conception of life" and "love of the romantic," we see a
break from the "old-fashioned" American novel as Norris
closely describes the details of Polk Street. While flawed
by the sentimentality of the Grannis-Baker episodes, the
anticlimatic conclusion, and especially by Norris's tight
focus on the negative aspects of life, McTeague still presents an effective picture which has form, texture, and
color. "It abounds in touches of character at once fine
and free, in little miracles of observation, in vivid insight, in simple and subtle expression."

27 "An Idyl of San Francisco," Argonaut, XLV (October 16), 9.
Norris will not fail "to write a great novel for lack of
trying many fields." After a sea story and a "Zolaesque
tragedy," he has now written a charming love idyll. Blix
interestingly reveals Norris's knack for story telling, but
it is marred by his misunderstanding of life in high society.
Blix has not yet "come out," yet she attends all of the
social functions. She entertains Condy at home, alone--
something a girl in her social class would not do.

28 "Literary Chat," Munsey's Magazine, XX (January), 653.
Moran of the Lady Letty "goes at a sure, strong pace."
Its "strange, picturesque events" are related with sincer-
ity and vigor. Norris has made a good beginning.

29 "Literary Notes," Washington Times (July 16), pt. 2, p. 18.
Announcement that the author of McTeague has left San
Francisco for the San Joaquin Valley "to work upon a new
novel for which he has made some elaborate plans."

1899

30   "Literature," The Independent, L (October 20), 1129.
          Moran of the Lady Letty is a romance reminiscent of the
     work of Bret Harte, Stevenson, Joaquin Miller, and Charles
     William Stoddard. Its tone is amateurish; but the story is
     not ill-told and may be enjoyed by those who do not insist
     upon "finished" art. "If the author is young we may yet
     have good work from him."

31   "Literature", The Independent, LI (April 6), 968.
          McTeague possesses "dramatic power of a rude sort," but
     "no person will be the better for reading it." It contains
     no moral, esthetic, or artistic qualities.

32   LUMMIS, CHARLES F. "Another California Novel," Land of Sunshine,
     XI (July), 117.
          The "hideous" and "haunting" story of McTeague is a
     "human document, a fine and powerful piece of work." Though
     Marcus is more a caricature than a character, and Grannis
     and Baker are Dickensian exaggerations, the other characters
     are very well drawn. The plot is firmly developed. It is
     not the best recent California novel, but all Californians
     should be proud of Norris's achievement.

33   LUMMIS, CHARLES F. "Another Success By Norris," Land of Sun-
     shine, XI (November), 353.
          Blix is "almost the swing of the pendulum from McTeague,"
     and while it is not so powerful, its "direct, simple, yet
     ingenious" style is far more comfortable to read. The de-
     scriptions are "unusually good" and the characterizations
     are "literally excellent."

34   M. "The Book and the Public," Pacific Monthly, VIII (December),
     24-25.
          Blix is an "entertaining little book", quite unlike the
     horribly realistic McTeague. There is, however, a great
     flaw to be noted: Norris gives Blix eyes that twinkle,
     thus suggesting the eyes of rodents. Since Norris has no
     sense of the fitness of things, he should cease writing.

35   [MARCOSSON, ISAAC F.] "Blix And Her Story," Louisville Times
     (November 13), p. 6.
          Marcosson praises Moran of the Lady Letty and McTeague,
     notes how different they are from each other, and relates
     how Blix is yet another work of a totally different char-
     acter. It is a "glorious," "keen," and "vivid" story which
     thrills without employing "silly sentimentality." Norris's
     characters are "actual people" and his language seems "to
     be forged with gleaming steel." He is "the American real-
     ist."

36   [MARCOSSON, ISAAC F.] "The Story of McTeague," Louisville
        Times (March 13), p. 6.
            Moran of the Lady Letty led us to expect much from Norris.
        The "strong, virile" McTeague, "throbbing with life, and
        brutally lifelike," fulfills our expectations. It is a
        "harsh, uncompromising study of humanity," vividly told in
        the realistic vein. At the same time it contains real senti-
        ment and humor. McTeague is "a distinct advance in art."

37   "McTeague", The Academy, LVII (December 23), 746.
            In Shanghaied Norris exhibited "a genuine imaginative
        talent." In McTeague he has used this strength "brutally."
        No sordid detail or "revolting episode" is omitted from his
        description of "nether San Francisco." Norris should in-
        clude something of the ideal in his vision; it should "com-
        prise something beyond the gross animalism of humanity."

38   "McTeague," The Literary Era, VI (June), 178.
            Though harsh and even brutal at times, McTeague is a
        "powerful and forceful" novel envincing "something nearly
        akin to genius." The curse of money has perhaps never been
        so "overwhelmingly" depicted.

39   "McTeague," The Literary News, XX (April), 109.
            Reprint of "A New And Promising American Novelist"
        (1899.41).

40   "'McTeague,'" Saturday Review (London), LXXXVIII, Supplement
        D9 (December 9), 14.
            In McTeague Norris has written a "social study" of human
        nature in its sordid and brutal aspects. Norris could not
        have created "more unpleasant characters," and the result
        is an unrelieved drab monotone.

41   "A New And Promising American Novelist," New York Tribune:
        Illustrated Supplement (March 5), p. 14B.
            Like other "slum novels," McTeague is "more repellant"
        than fiction should be. Yet, in this tale of the effects
        of greed, Norris's "untutored talent," vigor, and sincerity
        lead one to expect "strong work from him in the future."
        While Norris is sometimes excessive, one can see from his
        characterization of McTeague that he has "merits of an un-
        common sort."

42   "A New 'Great American Novel,'" Buffalo Morning Express (March
        12), p. 18.
            McTeague is an episodic tale, reminiscent of Stephen
        Crane's sketches. It has its weaknesses, especially in

its plot, but also its strengths, which lie in photographic rendering of particulars, and humor. McTeague reveals Norris's vitality and originality, and he should do better in his next book.

43 "Novels and Tales," The Outlook, LXI (March 18), 646-47.
McTeague is faithful to life, sincerely told, and reveals "distinct power." But it is unfortunate that Norris should spend his skills on a portrait of life "so essentially without spiritual significance." Though there is a "touch of idealism" in the Grannis-Baker affair, must of the novel consists of "bold and brutal realism." "This is a serious artistic defect." Norris should blend the coarse and fine aspects of life, as does Rudyard Kipling.

44 "Novels Of The Week," New York Commercial Advertiser (September 23), p. 11.
Norris's novels abound "in the unexpected." He has followed the "slap-dash" romance of Moran of the Lady Letty and McTeague's "relentless tale of sordid life" with a "refreshing idyl of contemporary life." Blix is "one of the brightest and most enjoyable novels of the month."

45 "Novels Of The Week," Spectator, LXXXII (March 18), 386.
Shanghaied is "a strange tale...which reminds one in its main motive of Mr. Kipling's Captains Courageous."

46 "Novels Of The Week", Spectator, LXXXIII (November 4), 662.
McTeague is "a robust, but extraordinarily repulsive story of low life. ... The brutality of some scenes is quite indescribable." Norris showed some promise in Shanghaied, but now he is simply "an animal painter" who too often turns the stomach.

47 "Novels That Are Being Talked About," Publishers' Weekly, LV (May 27), 840.
Norris has followed Moran of the Lady Letty with the "much talked about" McTeague. Norris belongs to the realistic school, and "his Zola-like touches leave nothing unknown of the repulsiveness of his subject."

48 "A Rough Novel," Boston Evening Transcript (March 22), p. 10.
The reviewer is offended by McTeague's morbid contemplation of those things from which culture ought to have enfranchised us." He believes that no one could enjoy the "disgusting episodes," one of which "transcends anything yet perpetrated" by the realistic school.

49   SANBORN, ANNIE W.   "Books," Saint Paul Pioneer Press (October 1),
     p. 18.
         Sanborn notes the difference between the romance of Moran
     of the Lady Letty and the realism of McTeague, and how Blix
     presents a new kind of realism which is idealistic and invig-
     orating. Although Blix is not without "some incongruities,
     even some cheapness," it freshly and vividly depicts the
     effects of virtuous living.

50   "Shanghaied," The Academy, LVI (March 18), 328.
         Shanghaied is "incisively written."

51   "Shanghaied," The Bookman (English), XVI (April), 22.
         Shanghaied is a "stirring tale well told." Moran, a
     "modern Amazon," is a "highly original conception"; Kitchell
     is fascinating. "We shall await Mr. Norris's next work with
     much interest."

52   "Shanghaied," The Daily Telegraph (London) (April 7), p. 3.
         Shanghaied is a "delightful" novel, "fresh, breezy, orig-
     inal, and full of interest." Norris exhibits "vivid descrip-
     tive power." Especially good is the description of the dead
     Moran being carried out to sea.

53   "Shanghaied," North British Daily Mail (Glasgow) (April 10),
     p. 2.
         Not many novels thrill the reader as Shanghaied does.
     The "novel" incidents are "highly picturesque" and the style
     is "vigorous." Moran is boldly drawn. It is difficult to
     put the book down.

54   "'Shanghaied,'" Saturday Review (London), LXXXVII (June 3), 696.
         Shanghaied is a "skilfully told tale," but its clever-
     ness is too reminiscent of similar tales to be termed novel.
     One of the best things in the book is "the breezy sketch of
     the roaring skipper, Kitchell."

55   "Shanghaied," The Scotsman (Edinburgh) (April 6), p. 2.
         Shanghaied is "briskly and brightly told," and "thrilling
     incidents are crowded thick on a small canvas." Moran is a
     "strong and original character, powerfully depicted." With
     a "vigorous and terse style" Norris gives an air of reality
     to the improbable.

56   "'Shanghaied,'" The Star (London) (April 22), p. 1.
         Shanghaied is "a splendid sea story." Kitchell is a
     "delightful ruffian" and Moran is "one of the most original
     heroines in recent fiction."

1899

57   SHINN, CHARLES HOWARD. "Literature Of The Pacific Coast," The
        Forum, XXVIII (October), 256.
              Moran of the Lady Letty, "a vivid tale of adventure, is
        still a growing success." Though Norris has been told "by
        more than one reviewer that the closing chapers...are un-
        satisfactory...it is hard to overpraise" the character of
        Moran and the fight at Magdalena Bay. Norris's latest
        book, McTeague, contains "nothing equal to the best episodes"
        of Moran of the Lady Letty.

58   "A Story of San Francisco," New York Times: Saturday Review of
        Books and Art, XLVIII (March 11), 150. McTeague recalls the
        style and subject matter of George Moore's Esther Waters.
        Both works attempt to depict life precisely and provide a
        moral lesson by portraying the degeneration of an individual.
        McTeague's faults are a wearisome repetition of detail and a
        lack of "lugubrious" incidents--though the wedding supper
        scene indicates that Norris does not lack a sense of humor.
        Although the novel is "pretty hard reading and not a book
        to enjoy," it reveals a talent "that may turn out to be
        genius."

59   "Summer Reading," Review of Reviews (American), XIX (June),
        749.
              Very unlike the "original and wideawake" Moran of the
        Lady Letty, McTeague is "about the most unpleasant American
        story that anybody has ever ventured to write." But it
        shows more "power and directness of method" than Moran; and,
        hopefully, Norris will in the future use his talent to write
        books "that will not be less true but a good deal more
        agreeable."

60   "Talk About Books," The Chautauquan, XXX (December), 329.
              Blix is a "crisp little story" with "just enough plot
        to hold it together." It furnishes "an hour's excellent
        entertainment."

61   Van Westrum, A. Schade. "A Bundle of Good Stories," The Book
        Buyer, XIX (November), 298.
              Blix is a "clever" tour de force in which there are few
        traces of natural spontaneity. Norris is too obviously
        deliberate. His understanding of social life is crude and
        badly "jumbled." The disjointed dialogues reveal that, like
        the early Stephen Crane, Norris is "too conscientiously
        aiming at realism."

62   "Weekly Record Of Publications," Publishers' Weekly, LV (March
        18), 509.
              Norris depicts the "curse of greed" in McTeague with "the

brutal realism of Zola." Although there are a "few glimpses
of humor" in the scenes involving the Sieppes, the "serious
and tragic predominates."

63   "Weekly Record Of Publications," Publishers' Weekly, LVI (September 23), 388.
        Summarizes the story of Blix and notes that it is by the
author of McTeague.

64   "A Western Realist," Washington Times (April 23), p. 20.
        In McTeague, a "grewsome tale" of a "half human" hero and
various other "warped or distorted specimens of humanity,"
Norris exercises a power of description that is "something
marvelous, and his grasp of character [is] equally sure."
McTeague is not a tract on stinginess, as several reviewers
have claimed, but a portrait of the effects of heredity and
environment upon unfortunate individuals. Nothing stronger
"in the way of realistic fiction is to be found in American
literature," and while Norris is not a mere imitator, he
deserves to be called "the American Zola." He has given us
a novel that is absolutely "true to life."

1900

1   "Blix", The Academy, LVIII (May), 534.
        The happy idyll of Blix "makes for fun and happiness."

2   "Books Of The Week: Another Study Of 'Realism'--The Medical
Handbook in Fiction," Providence Journal (February 11),
p. 15.
        Like many realists, Norris pays much attention to tech-
nique but gives us little true-to-life "reality" in his
books. Thus, in A Man's Woman the reader finds the detailed
depiction of such things as Arctic suffering and hip surgery,
but the total picture of life given is unreal and distorted.
A Man's Woman, like McTeague, too often reads like a medical
text book.

3   "Books," St. Paul Pioneer Press (March 25), p. 23.
        A Man's Woman is a powerful, well constructed novel with
much psychological interest. Norris's realism is often too
strong--as in the descriptions of Arctic suffering and surg-
ery--and Norris pays too much attention to minute details of
everyday life. But, overall, A Man's Woman is a fine piece
of work. The characterizations are especially masterful.

1900

4   [COOPER, FREDERIC TABER.] "Literature, American and English,"
    The International Year Book: 1899. New York: Dodd, Mead &
    Company, 1900, p. 489.
        McTeague was "the only important representation of the
    realistic novel" produced in America in 1899.

5   FORD, JAMES L. "Pseudo-Realism," Providence Journal (February
    25), p. 15.
        Unlike Dickens, who knew how to blend pathos and humor,
    Norris can only pile horror upon horror in A Man's Woman,
    especially in the Arctic exploration and surgical scenes.
    While Norris does exhibit some real literary skill, he
    might better devote his energies to other kinds of work,
    such as "the preparation of catalogues of undertaker's
    supplies."

6   "Frank Norris's 'A Man's Woman,'" Argonaut, XLVI (March 12), 8.
        In A Man's Woman Norris focuses on a much-discussed con-
    temporary question: the problem of a husband and wife
    having separate careers. And he provides the standard sol-
    ution by having Lloyd give up hers for the sale of Ward's.
    Though there are vivid pictures of suffering and "life-like"
    descriptions of the commonplace, A Man's Woman is not pleas-
    urable to read. There is too much detail and wearisome
    psychologizing.

7   "Hints For Spring Reading," St. Louis Republic, Magazine Sec-
    tion (March 25), [p. 11.]
        Like Stephen Crane in The Monster, Norris can "reel off
    horrors," though he does exhibit real literary "virtues"
    in A Man's Woman. Unfortunately, Norris's heroine "is not
    a man's woman at all; she is too strong-minded." And the
    hero is not "a woman's man."

8   "Literary Notes," St. Paul Pioneer Press (March 5), p. 4.
        Reprints the first paragraph of "Books of the Week"
    (1900.2).

9   "Literary Notes," Washington Times (November 11), pt. 2., p. 8.
        An advance notice of The Octopus. Norris's life is out-
    lined and his compositional methods are described: Norris
    considers three thousand words a "fair day's task;" he
    "prunes and revises with infinite care;" he very carefully
    researches his subjects.

10 LUMMIS, CHARLES F. "Beauty And The Brute," Land of Sunshine,
    XII (May), 385.
        Because "more varied," A Man's Woman is a more satisfying
    book than McTeague or Blix. There is much originality in

the plot and vivid characterization. There is also much of
the grimness that one has come to expect of Norris. The
novel is "of very uncommon force."

11   [LUMMIS, CHARLES F.] "Frank Norris," Land of Sunshine, XIII
      (June), 18.
           Norris's masculine books deserve praise. Their quality
      gives promise of even greater future achievements.

12   "A Man's Woman," Academy and Literature, LIX (October 20), 362.
           "Readers of Shanghaied, McTeague, and Blix will follow
      Mr. Norris anywhere," even to the Arctic in A Man's Woman.
      "We have glanced at the end of the story; it is most quietly
      effective."

13   "A Man's Woman," Baltimore Sun (March 12), p. 10.
           A Man's Woman is a "strong story and a subtle one in some
      portions."

14   "'A Man's Woman,'by Frank Norris," Chicago Inter Ocean (March
      12), p. 4.
           After a brief summary of A Man's Woman, the reviewer de-
      clares it "a strong story, which resolves the unanswered
      problems in many a real life."

15   "A Man's Woman," The Bookman (English), XIX (December), 90-91.
           While A Man's Woman is "faulty in design," "uneven in its
      workmanship," and simply wrong in its claim that Lloyd is an
      ideal woman, it exhibits the saving grace of Norris's char-
      acteristic individuality. The hero and heroine are "finely
      conceived and finely drawn." Norris excels in the depiction
      of abnormal types.

16   "A Man's Woman," Boston Evening Transcript (March 21), p. 12.
           Although Howells thinks that Norris "has arrived," A
      Man's Woman reveals that Norris lacks the essential quality
      of a great writer: "a sense of harmony, proportion and
      atmosphere." He lacks style and "the perception that truth
      and beauty are one."

17   "A Man's Woman," The Independent, LII (March 8), 611.
           A Man's Woman is not literature, but the story telling
      is excellent--until the conclusion. Then it is weakened by
      the "strained sentimental attitude" of the heroine. Norris
      has "a fine genius, which makes itself distinctly felt."

1900

18   "A Man's Woman," Literary World, XXXI (July 1), 140.
     The reviewer characterizes A Man's Woman as Norris's
     attempt at "'piling on the agony.'" He lists several such
     aspects of the story and concludes, "such incidents warn
     the reader what to expect."

19   "Man's Woman, A," The Outlook, LXIV (March 3), 486.
     A Man's Woman is a decided advance over McTeague in the
     development of character, and Norris handles his story with
     "distinct power." But, as in McTeague, Norris again presents
     "a most repellant and brutal" tale of human suffering. The
     surgical scene is "sickening and disgusting." Norris "out-
     Zolas Zola" in this instance.

20   "A Man's Woman," Overland Monthly, XXXV (May), 476.
     There is much strength in A Man's Woman, but also much
     unnecessary brutality. Even though the novel suffers from
     grotesque exaggerations of reality, it is still "intensely
     thrilling and exciting."

21   "A Man's Woman," Public Opinion, XXVIII (March 1), 281-82.
     Although there are touches of "ultra-realism" in A Man's
     Woman, it is not a "realistic" novel. But as one reads its
     gripping story, he ceases to care to what school it belongs.
     Especially masterful is the crucial point of the story--when
     Ward prevents Lloyd from going to Ferriss. After reading
     this scene all of the minor weaknesses of the novel are for-
     gotten.

22   "'A Man's Woman,'" San Francisco Chronicle (February 16), p.
     24.
     Though the crucial incident of A Man's Woman is not cred-
     ible, the rest of the novel is. It moves forward strongly,
     "with the sureness of fate." It evidences Norris's genius
     for "putting things in a way that scar them into the mem-
     ory." It is the best work he has yet done.

23   "A Man's Woman," New Orleans Times-Picayune (April 8), pt. 3,
     p. 7.
     The characters and incidents of A Man's Woman are "un-
     real," and its story contains "a good deal of sheer, incon-
     siderate brutality." But Norris's stylistic and character-
     ization abilities command the reader's interest from the
     first page on.

24 "McTeague," The Bookman (English), XVII (January), 121.
   One reads the story of McTeague with an interest that in-
   creases up to the climax. The hero is drawn "with a bold and
   masterly hand;" and every other character "lives." Norris
   has struck a perfect balance between romance and realism.

25 "Mr. Norris's Ultra Realism," New York Times: Saturday Review
   of Books and Art, XLIX (February 10), 82.
   A Man's Woman is a "strong and original book" but is
   flawed by a hero of monstrous appearance, a masculine heroine, and Norris's abandoning of the only noble character,
   Ferriss, half way through the story. Moreover, Norris too
   often makes "your flesh creep." The beginning of the tale
   is a "skillful mosaic of the worst sufferings of various
   expeditions" to the Arctic. Hip surgery is described "with
   a minuteness that is simply sickening." And after the surgery we go on to see a horse brained with a hammer. A
   novel should not be "a chamber of horrors nor a surgical
   journal."

26 "The New American Novelist," Washington Times (February 18),
   pt. 2, p. 8.
   Norris's work has been wide in range, finished in style,
   and original in every way. He has a brilliant future before
   him, but it will be a matter of opinion as to whether or
   not A Man's Woman establishes his "greatness." In some ways
   A Man's Woman is not so good as McTeague, but it is more
   subtle and profound. Also, it is more ambitious than the
   sea adventure of Moran of the Lady Letty and the love idyll
   of Blix. Norris is at his best in his portrayal of Lloyd,
   which reveals "a subtle and quick intuition and depth of
   insight which is rare among novelists."

27 "Notes of a Novel Reader," The Critic, XXXVI (April), 352-53.
   With an "improbable" hero, an "impossible" heroine, and
   an unimaginable situation, the last term to apply to A Man's
   Woman is "realistic." Yet, the story is "worth while."
   Norris grips one's attention and holds it tensely. Such
   power as Norris lavishly employs "is an exhilarating spec-
   tacle."

28 "Novels of the Week," Spectator, LXXXV (July 7), 19.
   From the "clash of arms" in McTeague and the "life of
   action" in Shanghaied, Norris has moved into the idyllic
   vein with Blix. It is "excellent in feeling and sincere in
   sentiment," and the "lapses from good taste are so surpris-
   ingly few and far between, when one remembers his last book,
   that we confidently look forward to the time when Mr. Norris
   will be wholly reconciled to the value of reticence."

1900

29   "Our Library Table," Athenaeum (October 27), p. 547.
            While A Man's Woman is carefully written, it is not pleas-
        ant reading. The "highstrung" characters experience enough
        crises "for half a dozen volumes," and an act of surgery is
        described with "painful minuteness."

30   "Shanghaied," Athenaeum (April 14), p. 461.
            Shanghaied is a typical, but vigorously well-told, adven-
        ture tale. However, it is difficult to believe that the
        hero could change so much while at sea and no longer care
        for civilization.

31   "Some American Heroines," The Academy, LIX (August 11), 111-12.
            Although Blix ends with "a most candid creak of optimis-
        tic machinery," Norris gives a very praiseworthy portrait
        of the American woman: "he is never tired of showing the
        strength of his visualization of this daughter of San Fran-
        cisco."

32   "Spring Flowers Of Fiction," The Book Buyer, XX (April), 237-38.
            A Man's Woman is a meritorious but disappointing book.
        Lloyd is hardly the ideal man's woman. There is too much
        brutality. The conclusion is "lurid melodrama, worthy of
        Sardou at his worst." Norris is a strong, "virile" writer
        and we still hope to someday see great things from him.

                                    1901

1   ALDEN, WILLIAM L. "London Letter," New York Times: Saturday
            Review of Books and Art, L (October 5), 722.
            Norris's Zolaesque The Octopus has made "a true literary
        sensation" in London. Reviewers have noted a few flaws in
        it, but "the real greatness of the book is gladly acknowl-
        edged" by all.

2   "The Book and the Public," Town Talk, IX (May 18), 24-25.
            The Octopus does not accurately represent the social
        status of the San Joaquin farmers, but it is a great book
        nonetheless. That it went into its second printing within
        four days after its publication may indicate that the read-
        ing public will always choose a good book when one is to
        be had.

3   The Bookworm. "A Great Novel," Town Talk, IX (April 20),
            25-26.
            The Octopus settles the question of whether or not Norris
        should be placed in the front rank of writers. It is an

"absorbing narrative" which accurately depicts the California
setting and the historical events that lie behind the tale.
All characters are distinctly depicted as individuals. Some
wonderfully "truthful" landscape descriptions are drawn by
Norris's "masterly hand." The only flaw to note is Norris's
habit of repetition.

4   "Book Reviews," Canadian Magazine, XVII (August), 392-93.
        The Octopus is "well called an epic." Although Norris is
    sometimes "rather discursive," his powers of description are
    remarkable. The tragedy is relieved by "some bright pictures
    of California and western humor."

5   COOPER, FREDERIC TABER. " Frank Norris's 'The Octopus,'" The
    Bookman (American), XIII (May), 245-47.
        With A Man's Woman and The Octopus Norris has successively
    moved farther away from real life than he was in McTeague.
    In The Octopus he has substituted types for individuals and
    fully moved into the realm of allegory. Yet the novel's
    epical structure and verbal power compel us to respond pos-
    itively. And we also find ourselves admiring the way in
    which the two main aspects of the theme are "kept before
    the reader, like the constantly recurring motivs of a
    Wagnerian opera."

6   "An Epic of Wheat," Overland Monthly, XXXVII (May), 1050-51.
        Norris portrays the basic qualities of human nature in
    The Octopus with the bold strokes of Zola and Hugo. In the
    Vanamee-Angèle subplot he employs the "most modern psychol-
    ogical thought." Norris is easily the peer of Kipling: in
    fact, it is doubtful that Kipling could write a novel that
    equals The Octopus's "handling of the complex forces of
    modern life, creation of character, or realism." One may
    not agree with the novel's conclusion, but Norris's ability
    as a writer must be recognized.

7   "The Epic of the Wheat," Boston Evening Transcript (May 22)
    p. 18.
        In The Octopus Norris has given us not "A Story of Cal-
    ifornia," but a "story of the world," of a "vast and terr-
    ible conflict of powers, symbolizing the whole of the strug-
    gle for existence." It represents a Zolaesque striving for
    "the light" through the character of Presley. "Mr. Norris
    had done his best" in one of the finest novels of the year.

1901

8   FITCH, GEORGE HAMLIN. "Books For Spring," San Francisco Chron-
       icle (April 7), p. 28.
          The Octopus is the strongest work Norris has yet written.
       Exhibiting a Zolaesque attention to detail, a Kiplingesque
       virility of style, and a sense of economy in description
       and dialogue that reminds one of Hamlin Garland's work, it
       provides an unforgettable experience for the reader. It is
       "full of the vitality of real life."

9   [HOWELLS, WILLIAM DEAN.] "Editor's Easy Chair," Harper's Monthly,
       CIII (October), 824-25.
          The Octopus is flawed by a tendency toward melodrama and
       unnecessary repetition of detail. But it is still "a great
       book," an epic of "Zolaesque largeness." Norris's descrip-
       tions of the "stir of dumb cosmic forces" are "of great im-
       aginative consequence" and his characterizations are in every
       sense realistic.

10   "Huntington, In A Novel That Pictures The Part The Southern Pac-
       ific Played In The Grim Tragedy Of Mussel Slough," San
       Francisco Examiner (April 6), p. 3.
          A sensational, full-page resume of The Octopus in which
       the reviewer quotes profusely. The reviewer celebrates the
       muckraking, rather than literary, value of the novel.

11   "Literary Notes," Washington Times (March 24), pt. 2, p. 10.
          Quotes an advance notice on the subject matter of The
       Octopus: it will deal with the "Mussel Slough Affair."

12   "Literary Review for 1901," The Current Encyclopedia, I (Sep-
       tember 15), 367.
          Norris's exposure of social inequity in The Octopus is
       "powerful, painstaking and realistic." The "crude power"
       of his Zolaesque style is unequaled by any contemporary
       writer.

13   LONDON, JACK. "The Octopus," Impressions Quarterly, II (June)
       46.
          In The Octopus the "promise of Moran of the Lady Letty
       and McTeague has been realized." Like Presley, Norris has
       sought to capture the essence of the West, and he has ad-
       mirably succeeded. Embracing an economic interpretation of
       history, Norris has written an epic of the machine age. The
       only flaw to be noted in The Octopus is the "inordinant real-
       ism" Norris exhibits when too minutely rendering petty de-
       tails. But this is forgotten when the reader encounters
       strong characterizations like that of Annixter and the vivid
       descriptions of nature. (For a full description of this
       review, see Isani [1973.3].)

14 LUMMIS, CHARLES F. "That Which Is Written," Land of Sunshine,
   XV (July), 58.
      Powerful and surprising as they were, Norris has raised
   his sights above McTeague and A Man's Woman in The Octopus.
   While Norris's character drawing is not very skillful and
   he is "too diligently brutal in style," his novel possesses
   "tremendous strength." Norris has truly and vividly depicted
   an historical event. Such grasp, force, and depth very few
   "American authors can either summon or harness" as success-
   fully as Norris has.

15 [MARCOSSON, ISAAC F.] "The Epic Of The Wheat," Louisville Times
   (April 13), p. 13.
      All of the characters of The Octopus are unerringly drawn.
   It is a "tragically serious" story of the oppressor and the
   oppressed, a mighty novel capturing all aspects of human existence in the most realistic terms.

16 "Minor Fiction," Washington Times (March 10), pt. 2, p. 10.
      Advance announcement of The Octopus: it will focus on
   the relations between the railroad and the wheat growers of
   California, and "may go further to make Mr. Norris, dealing
   with modern California wheat, what Bret Harte was to the
   early gold country."

17 MC GAFFEY, ERNEST. "The Frank Norris I Know," Chicago American:
   Art and Literary Review (April 20), p. 1.
      Norris "has, to the very core, those essentials which go
   to make up a real writer." He is a great lover of nature,
   who brings "an almost brush-like effect to his pen strokes
   in painting the titanic scenery of the West." His work
   shows a constant improvement in power and breadth.

18 "The Novel of the West," Washington Times (June 2), pt. 2, p. 8.
      Some of those who read Norris's earlier romances prophesied
   that he would produce great work some day. The Octopus is
   not a pleasant book, but Norris has eliminated the more
   clumsy features of his style and produced a great story.
   As was seen in McTeague, Norris is both a realist and a poet,
   and he brings all of his strengths to bear in The Octopus.

19 "The Octopus," Academy and Literature, LXI (September 7), 193.
      An attempt at summary by a reviewer who has not read The
   Octopus: "the Octopus is a tract of country in California....
   Mr. Norris gives a very business-like air to this novel by
   including a map of the Octopus district."

1901

20 "The Octopus," Athenaeum (October 5), 447-48.
McTeague and Blix have given Norris "some standing" in
England, but no one was prepared for "so important a piece
of work" as The Octopus. Although "not a fully formed work,"
flawed as it is by "overfluency," "lack of restraint," a
tautology, and an unnecessary resume in chapter five, it
remains a "powerful and tragic piece of fiction."

21 "The Octopus," The Independent, LIII (May 16), 1139-40.
The Octopus dramatizes a tragic situation in a way that
enlarges the reader's view of life. Because of its many
fine elements the book stands well above "the rank of common-
place fiction." Unfortunately it is flawed by Norris's lack
of restraint.

22 "Octopus (The): A Story of California," The Outlook, LXVII
April 20), 923-24.
"Following Zola in his great trilogy of Paris life,"
Norris has begun his trilogy of the wheat with a "vivid,
dramatic narrative." Norris's portrait is broad and compre-
hensive, and at the same time, minutely realistic--sometimes
annoyingly so. Also annoying is Norris's Wagner-like habit
of repeatedly reiterating the typical traits of his characters. Happily, there is less brutality in The Octopus than
in Norris's previous works. As a whole, the novel is "extraordinary" in its grasp of life.

23 "The Octopus: A Story of California," Spectator, LXXX (October
5), 486.
The Octopus is an "exceedingly interesting book," present-
ing a conflict between the "old civilization of the ranch"
and the "new enterprise of the railway contractor." It is
full of moving incidents, vivid description, passion, and
pathos. If Norris is "sometimes a little too hot and heavy,
it must be recognized that, on the other hand, he is never
dull."

24 "The Octopus", Review of Reviews (English), XXIV (October), 423-
24.
The Octopus is a story of "unadulterated horror", a "trag-
edy in which the economic forces reign supreme." It is "the
Greek drama" of Aeschylus "re-dressed as a modern novel."
With the "straining rhetoric" of Hugo and the method of
Zola, Norris depicts a "hideous nightmare" with extraordinary
power.

25 "The Octopus," The World's Work, II (May), 782.
       Although a note of "immaturity" is occasionally heard,
    The Octopus is "of special interest and merit." In a force-
    ful style, Norris makes an unusual blend of "realism, mysti-
    cism, idealism, pessimism, and optimism," and the result is a
    very convincing point of view on the struggle between the
    farmers and the railroad in the San Joaquin Valley.

26 PAYNE, WILLIAM MORTON. "Recent Fiction," The Dial, XXXI (Sep-
       tember 1), 136.
       Norris's "brutal realism" in his earlier works matched
    that of Zola; and in The Octopus Norris has attempted to
    equal the scope of Zola's work. Although he is "essentially
    inartistic" in his heavy-handed Zolaesque methods, Norris
    does win our admiration and respect because of his "inten-
    sity of feeling" and "vivid" depictions. Unfortunately, the
    virulence and single-mindedness of his attack on the rail-
    road is unacceptable, and we find ourselves siding with the
    villain Norris has drawn.

27 "The Promise of a Great Story," Argonaut, XLVII (May 13), 8.
       The Octopus lacks a fully realized "outline and perspect-
    ive"; Norris has not "yet learned the secrets of harmony in
    color." The idea of the book and its many truthful, stirring,
    and pathetic elements are praiseworthy, though; and when the
    Great American Novel is written it will be along the lines
    that Frank Norris has attempted."

28 RICE, WALLACE. "Norris's 'The Octopus,'" Chicago American:
    Literary and Art Review (April 6), pp. 5-6.
       The Octopus is a "fascinating" novel, but is flawed by
    repetitiveness and lack of structure. It also suffers from
    too much clever literary manipulation, lapses in realism,
    and Norris's irresponsible philosophic vision (as it is
    expressed by Shelgrim). (For a full discussion of this
    review, see Davison [1968.3].)

29 "Talk About Books," The Chautauquan, XXXIII (August), 539.
       The Octopus is "worthy of commendation" as an attempt to
    depict the meaning of life in the West and as a critique of
    mercantile culture. The characters are vitally drawn, yet
    we cannot accept Norris's transformation of the ranchers
    into criminals. Surely the relation between producer and
    transporter is different from Norris's portrait of it.

1901

30 "The Trilogy of Wheat," The Bookman (American), XIII (May),
    212-13.
        Under the influence of Zola, Norris has begun a trilogy
    of wheat with a highly symbolical novel. If Norris only had
    as much experience as Zola, The Octopus might have come close
    to being the "Great American Novel."

31 VAN WESTRUM, A. SCHADE. "A Novelist With A Future," The Book
    Buyer, XXII (May), 326-28.
        Blix and A Man's Woman disappointed the expectations given
    rise by McTeague, but Norris has redeemed himself with The
    Octopus. Zolaesque in its scope and method, the novel is a
    very ambitious one, and it succeeds to a large degree. Its
    flaws are those which result from a young man's lack of
    experience. Norris promises much for the future and we are
    "beholden to him for the novel of the season."

32 "A Wheat Trilogy," Munsey's Magazine, XXV (August), 760.
        The Octopus reveals that Norris has grown remarkably
    since the days of McTeague. The villainy of the railroad
    is too melodramatically drawn and the style is sometimes
    too affected, but The Octopus is still a "human drama of a
    high type."

33 WILLIAMS, TALCOTT. "Fiction Read And Written In 1901", Review
    of Reviews (American), XXIV (November), 589-91.
        In a Zolaesque manner The Octopus illustrates the present
    tendency in literature to directly and honestly handle any
    subject. Though it is flawed by too many coincidental
    events, The Octopus is a powerful book.

1902

1 ARMES, WILLIAM DALLAM. "Concerning the Work of the late Frank
   Norris," Sunset, X (December), 165-67.
        Armes, a Berkeley professor, recalls Norris submitting
   one of the most vividly written, though unfinished, essays
   he had ever received. Reviewing Norris's life's work, he
   finds that Norris never changed. While his books were
   powerfully energetic, accurate to a fault, and vividly ren-
   dered, Norris never eliminated the crudities of his style.
   He never learned to revise.

2 "The Author and the Day's Work," The Bookman (American), XVI
   (December), 319-20.
        Passing reference to Norris having written McTeague in
   eighty-nine days.

3   "The Book and the Public," Town Talk, X (June 28), 24–25.
        Although Norris does not exactly render California his-
    tory in The Octopus, it is a "great book." Despite Norris's
    "dragging in of Tolstoi and Zola," The Octopus is a novel
    "that stands alone and needs no bolstering."

4   BOYNTON, HENRY W. "Literature and Fiction," Atlantic Monthly,
    LXXXIX (May), 708–09.
        The Octopus is pretentiously executed in the "realistic"
    manner. For instance, the descriptions of Hilma's appear-
    ance echo D'Annunzio and those of her odors recall "the sort
    of romantic vulgarity of which only the realist of the French
    school is capable." Yet, Norris's real power is revealed in
    his ability to capture "breathing human nature" in his char-
    acters.

5   COOPER, FREDERIC TABER. "Frank Norris," The Bookman (American),
    XVI (December), 334–35.
        The death of Zola's "most earnest desciple" is lamentable.
    Although The Octopus was a disappointment and McTeague was
    flawed by its conclusion, Norris's achievement in The Pit
    obliges us to admit that his death was "a serious loss to
    American letters."

6   [COOPER, FREDERIC TABER.] "Literature, American and English,"
    The International Year Book: 1901. New York: Dodd, Mead &
    Company, pp. 449, 452–53.
        Norris is one of the significant younger American writers
    who seek to "depict certain vital phases of typically Ameri-
    can life and character." The Octopus is one of the "boldest"
    efforts of 1901 to portray what is representatively American.
    As in McTeague Norris follows the method of Zola by emphas-
    izing a thematically central symbol: the wheat symbolizes
    the notion of "American prosperity." Unfortunately, The
    Octopus falters because Norris's concern for "big central
    ideas" causes him to sacrifice "the human interest of the
    individual characters."

7   "Death Ends the Career of Frank Norris," San Francisco Chronicle
    (October 26), 24.
        Laments the death of Norris as "a genuine loss to American
    literature," and recounts the details of Norris's life.
    McTeague and The Octopus are his most ambitious works. The
    conclusion of McTeague is especially powerful.

1902

8 "The Death of Mr. Frank Norris," The World's Work, V (December)
   2830.
        Norris had a steadfast resolve never to compromise him-
   self. He could have made more money by "writing sensational
   books, but he worked on, year after year, unswerving and
   content with the nobler aim."

9 "Death Stills the Pen of Frank Norris," San Francisco Examiner
   (October 26), p. 18
        Norris's death is a great loss to American literature.

10 FLOWER, B. O. "The Trust In Fiction: A Remarkable Social Novel,"
   The Arena, XXVII (May), 547-54.
        The Octopus is a vivid, distinctly great "novel of Ameri-
   can life" told with "marvelous insight" and accuracy. It
   exhibits Norris's broad philosophical grasp and Zolaesque
   passion for justice--so much so that it must also be termed
   a great "social study." It is a "work of genius."

11 "Frank Norris on the Responsibilities of the Novelist," Literary
   Digest, XXV (December 20), 831-32.
        Summarizes two of Norris's critical essays: "The Respon-
   sibilities of the Novelist," and "A Neglected American Epic."

12 "Frank Norris's Last Work," Argonaut, LI (November 10), 289-90.
        Observes that the last work of the late Norris appeared
   in Argonaut, as did some of his earliest works.

13 "From One Who Knows," Town Talk, X (June 28), 26.
        Recounts Norris's declaration in the second "Salt and
   Sincerity" essay that library book purchases are not det-
   rimental to an author's income.

14 GOODRICH, ARTHUR. "Frank Norris," Current Literature, XXXIII
   (December), 764.
        In "The Pit" Norris "has vivified his perfect realism by
   a creative imagination truer than that of The Octopus or
   McTeague." Norris's last story assures him a place in American literary history.

15 ____. "Frank Norris: The Estimate and Tribute of an Associate,"
   Boston Evening Transcript (October 29), p. 14.
        Laments Norris's death as a loss to American letters.

16 HOWELLS, WILLIAM DEAN. "Frank Norris," North American Review,
   CLXXV (December), 769-78.
        Deriving his ideal of the novel from Zola, Norris wrote
   two great "epical" books, McTeague and The Octopus. Though
   McTeague is flawed by Norris's penchant for melodrama, it

still manages to intensely capture reality throughout. Only
The Octopus surpasses McTeague's power. Its Homeric breadth,
vigorous action, strong characterizations, and its blend of
essential earthiness with the mythical make it "unequalled
for scope and for grasp" in American fiction. Norris was
one of the true pioneers of serious literature in America.

17 MILLARD, BAILEY. "Writer Was Planning to Stay in California
    This Winter and Complete 'The Wolf' When Stricken by Ap-
    pendicitis," San Francisco Examiner (October 26), p. 18.
        Norris followed many masters in his career: Kipling,
    Stevenson, Zola; but death came when he had finally over-
    come the influence of these other writers and was at last
    striking out on his own.

18 MUZZEY, A. L. "Book Notices," The Public, V (May 3), 64.
        If the rest of the trilogy sustains the power exhibited
    in The Octopus, it will place Norris in the ranks of the
    greatest novelists. Muzzey praises its vivid characteri-
    zations, the "photographic clearness" of its scenic descrip-
    tions, and the "burning earnestness" of its morality. He
    is surprised that it has not attracted wider attention
    from reviewers.

19 "Norris Died Intestate: Royalties in His Books His Principal
    Estate," San Francisco Chronicle (November 7), p. 14.
        In a petition for administration of Norris's estate,
    Mrs. Jeannette Norris declared that Norris died intestate.
    His estate consisted of one thousand dollars and the royal-
    ties for his books.

20 "'The Octopus: A Story of California,'" Saturday Review (Eng-
    lish), XCIII (March 8), 304.
        The Octopus awakens sympathies for the victims of the
    railroad, but Norris "leaves an impression of the inevita-
    bility of the series of tragedies which he describes." His
    style "lacks reserve;" his words "rage with cyclonic fury."
    How realistic the book is must be determined by those fa-
    miliar with California.

21 TODD, FRANK M. "Frank Norris--Student, Author, and Man," The
    University of California Magazine, VIII (November), 349-56.
        Todd, a friend of Norris since their days together at
    Berkeley, laments the death of Norris's "fine, brave spirit."
    He watched Norris grow from an unexceptional writer to a
    great one, a "genius of commanding force." Todd describes
    at length Norris's personality at Berkeley and Harvard, and
    celebrates his ability to write powerful stories.

1902

22　"An Unfinished Literary Career," Literary Digest, XXV (November
　　　8), 593.
　　　　　Quotes obituaries of Norris.

23　WOOD, WILLIAM ALLEN.　"A Golden Bowl Broken," Phi Gamma Delta
　　　Quarterly, XXV (December), 157-63.
　　　　　Summarizes and evaluates Norris's work.　Concludes that
　　　he was a "literary giant."　Presents much biographical data.

24　WRIGHT, H. M.　"In Memorian--Frank Norris:　1870-1902," The Uni-
　　　versity of California Chronicle, V (October), 240-45.
　　　　　Wright laments the death of his "very dear college friend."
　　　He outlines Norris's life:　his early bent toward painting,
　　　his keen interest in medieval French culture, his dislike
　　　for academic studies at Berkeley except for courses in French
　　　literature and two courses taught by Joseph Le Conte, and
　　　his choice of writing as his profession.

1903

1　AIKEN, CHARLES S.　"Books and Writers," Sunset, X (January), 245.
　　　　　The West feels the loss of Norris.　His essays for The
　　　Wave were the witty and insightful work of "a prophet with
　　　honor."　Norris's aim was to realistically depict the West
　　　and he did it "wondrously and peculiarly" well.

2　"American Literature," Saturday Review (English), XCV (February
　　　14), 206.
　　　　　Although The Pit is a superior novel, a "graphic and
　　　powerful study" of Chicago life, Norris was still too much
　　　under the influence of Zola and still too young to succeed
　　　in the grand plan of his trilogy.

3　BACON, THOMAS.　"The Last Book of Frank Norris," Impressions
　　　Quarterly, IV (March), 12.
　　　　　In The Pit Norris again illustrates his thesis that the
　　　forces of nature are inevitably stronger than the will of
　　　the individual, and he does so much more realistically than
　　　in The Octopus.　The characters of The Pit are especially
　　　true to life; and, while Laura is "uninteresting," Jadwin and
　　　Page are vividly drawn.

4　"Biographical Sketch of Frank Norris," Book News, XXI (February),
　　　443.
　　　　　Norris's death is a "severe loss to American literature."
　　　Had he continued to live he would have produced some "mighty"
　　　works; for, his last book, The Pit, exhibits a great advance
　　　over his previous work.

5   "Books of the Week," The Outlook, LXXV (October 10), 373.
          All of the stories in A Deal in Wheat exhibit a "Western
     flavor." The title story is a vigorous protest very much
     like that of The Pit, but it is hardly a "finished produc-
     tion." A much better story is "The Passing of Cock-Eye
     Blacklock."

6   BURGESS, GELETT.   "One More Tribute to Frank Norris," Sunset, X
     (January), 246.
          It was in 1897, when Norris was writing for The Wave, that
     his greatest growth as a writer took place. He then moved
     past the influence of Rudyard Kipling and Stevenson to dis-
     cover his own voice. While he always remained an unpolished
     writer, Norris became a very powerful story teller.

7   [COOPER, FREDERIC TABER.]   "Literature, American and English,"
     The International Year Book: 1902. New York: Dodd, Mead &
     Company, pp. 407, 408, 410.
          Norris was a young writer of great promise. More than any
     other writer he approached Zola's epic style. In The Octopus
     he symbolized American life in the figure of wheat; unfortu-
     nately, he emphasized the symbol to the degree that it marred
     the human interest of the book. In The Pit, however, Norris
     brought the symbolism of wheat under control, so that it was
     subordinate to the "interest of human characters."

8   COOPER, FREDERIC TABER.   "The Sustained Effort And Some Recent
     Novels," The Bookman (American), XVIII (November), 311-12.
          Norris could not be "hampered by a narrow canvas." It
     would be like setting Rodin "to carving cherry pits." Yet
     the stories of A Deal in Wheat are "full of the keenest in-
     terest." "A Memorandum Of Sudden Death" is Norris's nearest
     approach to "the artistic unity of the ideal short story;"
     it illustrates the length to which "occasional excesses of
     riotous romanticism would carry the author of Moran."

9   "A Deal In Wheat," Academy and Literature, LXV (November 7),
     500, 503.
          A Deal In Wheat is a collection of short stories told in
     Norris's characteristically vital style.

10   "A Deal in Wheat, and other Stories," Athenaeum (November 7),
     613.
          Were Norris alive he would not have published A Deal In
     Wheat. Though the stories are characteristically "muscular"
     and energetic, they are unoriginal and very much below the
     level of his best work.

1903

11 "A Deal in Wheat," Book News Monthly, XXII (October), 123.
    A Deal in Wheat contains stories of various phases of life
    drawn with "virility," "command of language," and a "wide
    knowledge of human nature and conditions."

12 "A Deal in Wheat," Current Literature, XXXIV (November), 626.
    A Deal in Wheat contains "strong, virile stories," compar-
    able to the works of Bret Harte and Rudyard Kipling.

13 "A Deal in Wheat," Literary News, XXIV (November), 322-23.
    A Deal in Wheat is another indication of how much American
    literature has lost with Norris's death. Again we see
    Norris's "power of vivid portraiture." These stories lack
    the "straining for effect" and "insistence on a particular
    point of view on a reader's part" that marred some of Norris's
    novels.

14 "A Deal in Wheat," London Times Literary Supplement (October 23)
    p. 304.
    At his best, Norris never escaped the influence of other
    writers. In A Deal in Wheat the sea stories are drawn from
    Stevenson's The Wrecker; and the best story, "The Passing of
    Cock-Eye Blacklock," is an unadulterated version of Lewis's
    Wolfville. "A Deal in Wheat" should have been thrown in the
    wastebasket. Norris's excellent McTeague and The Octopus are
    the books upon which his reputation must rest.

15 "An Epic Of The Wheat," Public Opinion, XXXIV (January 22), 121.
    The Pit is Norris's best book, a "great advance" over his
    previous work in that it is without excess. Norris exhibits
    a new "lightness of touch." He has admirably balanced the
    great with the minute, the tragic with the humorous.

16 "The Epic Of The Wheat," Literary Digest, XXVI (March 7), 353.
    Under the influence of Zola and Howells, Norris has pro-
    duced in The Pit "one of the strongest works of fiction" in
    recent American literary history.

17 "The Epic Of The Wheat--The Pit," Indianapolis News (January 10),
    p. 8.
    While in The Octopus we found Norris blending imagination
    with historical record, The Pit presents a fiction in which
    he fully expresses his imaginative powers. It is a "marvel-
    ous" story and an insightful "philosophical study of certain
    phases of American life." It not only captures the very at-
    mosphere of Chicago but the "bigness" of the American cont-
    inent and spirit. It thus "comes as near being the real
    American novel as any that has gone before."

18 F. C. B. "Talk About Books," The Chautauquan, XXXVII (April),
    100.
        Because they are such different books, it is difficult to
    tell whether The Octopus or The Pit is the better one. But
    we can say that stronger fiction than The Pit "has not been
    produced by writers of this generation in America."

19 FITCH, GEORGE HAMLIN. "Good Reading," San Francisco Chronicle
    (January 11), p. 18.
        The Pit is vastly superior to The Octopus. While The
    Octopus was a powerful book, it was flawed by tedious rep-
    etition of detail, the presence of characters who had no
    real bearing on the plot, and too much of the "grim and
    ghastly." The Pit contains none of these faults. All of
    the characters are true to life, and Jadwin and Laura are
    especially well drawn. The plot is handled effectively and
    the esoteric details of business in the Board of Trade are
    clearly communicated.

20 FLOWER, B. O. "The Pit," The Arena, XXIX (April), 440-42.
        Norris's "genius" promises to place him in the front rank
    of twentieth century American novelists. The Pit is a great
    novel, more finished and mature a work of art than The Oct-
    opus. But The Octopus is a better work because of its
    "dramatic force."

21 "Frank Norris; an Appreciation," New York Herald: Literary
    Section (March 1), p. 2.
        Laments Norris's death: "American literature [has] sus-
    tained one of the most serious losses known in its annals."
    The Octopus and The Pit reveal that Norris was just beginning
    to mature as an artist. With The Pit he began to move past
    his Zolaesque phase to assume his own distinctive voice.
    The Pit comes close to fulfilling the "Great American Novel"
    ideal.

22 "Frank Norris and Edwin Lefevre," The Bookman (American), XVI
    (January), 441-42.
        Anecdote about Norris's plan to have Lefevre check the
    details relating to wheat speculation in The Pit.

23 "Frank Norris," Literary News, XXIV (January), 9-10.
        Norris's death cut short a career of "Brilliant achieve-
    ment and measureless possibility." Norris stood "at the
    head" of those young writers who have focused on political,
    social, and economic realities. It was in The Octopus that
    Norris achieved his maturity as a novelist.

1903

24 "Frank Norris' Essays," <u>San Francisco Chronicle</u> (November 1),
    p. 8.
        The essays in <u>The Responsibilities of the Novelist</u> are
    strong, vigorous statements of the artistic creed that
    Norris illustrated in his works.

25 "Frank Norris' Short Stories," <u>San Francisco Chronicle</u> (November
    15), p. 8.
        The stories in <u>A Deal in Wheat</u> are all good, but will be
    forgotten while <u>The Octopus</u> and <u>The Pit</u> will be remembered.
    Like Zola, Norris needed a large canvas for his best work.
    Norris was not a short story writer at heart.

26 "Frank Norris's Last Novel," <u>Argonaut</u>, XLVIII (January 12), 23.
        Although flawed by a lack of suspense and Norris's de-
    cision not to conclude with the tragedy he led the reader to
    expect, <u>The Pit</u> is a "masterly work," filled with brilliant-
    ly described scenes. The most excellent thing in the book
    is the characterizations, from Jadwin to minor characters
    like Aunt Wess and Page. Norris also excels in capturing
    the subtle nuances of feminine conversation.

27 "Frank Norris's Latest Novel," <u>New York Evening Sun</u> (January 24),
    p. 5.
        <u>The Pit</u> reveals Norris's continued growth as a writer. He
    keeps his story "well under control," avoiding the excesses
    of his earlier work, and reaches "great heights of imagin-
    ative description."

28 "Frank Norris's 'The Pit,'" <u>The Bookman</u> (English), XXIII (March),
    246-47.
        While <u>The Octopus</u> presents the faults of a young writer,
    <u>The Pit</u> exhibits the skilled work of a mature artist "who
    pursues his idea in a straight line, gaining impetus and
    power with every page."

29 GARLAND, HAMLIN. "The Work of Frank Norris," <u>The Critic</u>, XLII
    (March), 216-18.
        In his masterworks--<u>McTeague</u>, <u>The Octopus</u>, and <u>The Pit</u>--
    Norris was not interested in being an "ethical teacher."
    Rather, he sought to capture reality. <u>McTeague</u> is "inexor-
    able in its unrelenting lifelikeness." In the frankly soci-
    ological <u>The Octopus</u>, Norris boldly depicted how individ-
    uals are determined by "blind forces." <u>The Pit</u> is a "superb
    study of Chicago on certain well-defined sides." Garland
    relates that he "saw a great deal" of Norris in Chicago as
    he was researching <u>The Pit</u>; he found him "boyish" and "fun-
    loving"--a side of his personality that was revealed only
    in <u>Blix</u>.

30 GOODRICH, ARTHUR. "Frank Norris, the Man," Current Literature,
        XXXIV (January), 105.
            Brief sketch of Norris's life. Goodrich praises Norris's
        high achievement.

31 HIGGINSON, THOMAS WENTWORTH, AND HENRY WALCOTT BOYNTON. A
        Reader's History of American Literature. Boston: Houghton
        Mifflin and Company, pp. 254-56.
            Like Hamlin Garland, Norris rebelled against the literary
        tradition of eastern America. But, unlike Garland, he went
        even farther east for his own literary models.

32 [HOWELLS, WILLIAM DEAN.] "Editor's Easy Chair," Harper's
        Monthly, CVI (January), 328.
            Norris understood the "divine secret of the supreme art-
        ists: he saw what was before him, with things in their
        organic relations, and he made life live." McTeague and
        The Octopus compare favorably with the "best of our time."

33 [HOWELLS, WILLIAM DEAN.] "The Last Work of Frank Norris,"
        Harper's Weekly, XLVII (March 14), 433.
            The Pit is a strong story which contains excellent char-
        acterizations and powerful dramatizations. But it follows
        "haltingly" upon The Octopus. The main flaw is Norris's
        lack of perspective. The courage and beauty of Jadwin and
        Laura apparently blinded Norris to their vulgarity.

34 JACKSON, F. "Editorial Digest," Overland Monthly, XLI (Feb-
        ruary), 153.
            The Pit depicts the various forces that are at work in
        creating American civilization of the future.

35 MABIE, HAMILTON W. "Studies in Literature," The Outlook, LXXV
        (December), 829-30.
            If Norris had not died, The Responsibilities of the Nov-
        elist would probably not have been published. The essays
        are fragmentary and brusque, written in newspaper style.
        But, though they are not of permanent value, they are inter-
        esting statements of a quickly growing young writer's ideals
        and his discontent with existing conditions in literature.

36 MARCOSSON, ISAAC F. "Frank Norris' Last Book," Louisville Times
        (January 3), section 2, p. 7.
            The Pit lacks the "heroic proportions" and "magnificent
        sweep" of The Octopus, but it is still a remarkable book.
        It is "more refined, more sustained art, at once appealing
        and impressive." Norris has succeeded in his plan to accur-
        ately depict a woman's nature. Norris's death is a great

loss. (Part of a letter from Norris to Marcosson—describing
The Pit—is reproduced.)

37 MILLARD, BAILEY. "Outline of 'The Pit,' Frank Norris' Last
and Best Novel," San Francisco Examiner (February 1), p. 10.
The Pit is a "strong, tense, colorful" romance. The
Octopus was tiresomely prolix, but The Pit proceeds quickly
from scene to scene. Laura is probably Norris's "best fem-
inine creation."

38 _____. "A Significant Literary Life," Out West, XVIII (January),
49-55.
Millard laments Norris's death and celebrates his achievement. While Norris's creations were "imperfectly individual-
ized," they were far better than the works of other writers
of his time. His books were often "morbid" and lacked
"spirituality;" and his frequent prolixity would have made
him unreadable had it not been that he imbued his stories
with a good deal of engaging action. Millard rates Moran of
the Lady Letty as Norris's best book because of its simplic-
ity and clarity.

39 "A Mine Of Thought," Public Opinion, XXXV (October 22), 536.
The essays in The Responsibilities of the Novelist reveal
Norris's inspiration and admirably high ideals as a writer.

40 "More Novels," Nation, LXXVI (April 2), 276.
The Pit is a "wondrously vivid" and "Hideously real" novel
which holds one's attention "like a vise." The characters
are well drawn, "in the style of ultra-detail."

41 "More of the Strenuous Life," Overland Monthly, XLI (February),
156-57.
The Pit is a story of "eager rushing, modern thought and
deed." Norris thrills us by showing the romance that lies
beneath the surface of everyday life.

42 "New Books," Washington Post (February 2), p. 7.
The Pit is a every engaging book. Albert Bigelow Paine's
censures (1903.44) are unnecessary.

43 "Norris—The Responsibilities of the Novelist," The Critic, XLIII
(December), 576.
The Responsibilities of the Novelist is Norris's sincere,
serious, unambiguous declaration of his opinions. Unfortunately, all of the essays included reveal that Norris made
"no effort to cultivate the essay as a literary form."

44 PAINE, ALBERT BIGELOW. "Frank Norris's 'The Pit,'" The Bookman
(American), XVI (February), 565–67.
   The Pit is "of less lavish conception" than The Octopus.
Yet, while it lacks the attractive "bigness" of The Octopus,
this powerful narrative is technically better and clearly
the "skilled work of the mature artist." (See "New Books"
[1903.42] for a rejoinder.)

45 PATTESON, MARY L. "'The Pit,'" New York Times: Saturday Review
of Books and Art, LII (March 7), 158.
   Rejoinder to "The Pit," (1903.47). In this letter to
the Times Patteson agrees with the reviewer that The Pit is
a lesser work than The Octopus, but disagrees with the conclusion that Norris should be faulted for his lack of finish.
She champions Norris as a Whitmanesque figure whose short-
comings were more than compensated for by his "forcefulness
of expression" and the important "message" he delivered.

46 PAYNE, WILLIAM MORTON. "Recent Fiction," The Dial, XXXIV (April
1), 242.
   The Pit's moral is nothing new. Charles Dudley Warner
and others have "preached effectively upon the same text."
As a novel it is not a success. Like The Octopus it is
"strained, turgid, and unconvincing."

47 "The Pit: A Dispassionate Examination of Frank Norris's Posthumous Novel," New York Times: Saturday Review of Books and
Art, LII (January 31), 66.
   Norris was a promising writer with great imaginative
ability and the power to accurately observe life. But, as
The Pit reveals, Norris never perfected his technical skills.
A "preacher turned novelist," he never gave finish to his
works. Consequently, his life's achievement is remarkable
rather than admirable. (See Patteson [1903.45] for a rejoinder.)

48 "The Pit," Athenaeum (February 14), 204–05.
   Norris's literary methods were Zolaesque and he took "no
account of literary niceties." He had a "fine feeling for
the bigness of things" that he expressed powerfully. The
Pit is a "very powerful melodrama," revealing that Norris
"had more in him than literary promise."

49 "The Pit," Book News Monthly, XXI (February), 437–38.
   A tremendous drama "is irresistably forced upon us" in
The Pit. Norris was a "Genius," a "brilliant novelist," and
in The Pit, an "elegant" stylist. His greatest talent was in
character creation: Laura is something new in the history
of women in fiction. Norris gives us more on one page than
can be gotten from hours of reading Henry James.

1903

50 "The Pit," Current Literature, XXXIV (March), 371.
   The characters of The Pit are "drawn finely and firmly,
   and with rare insight." The story is a "vigorous" one,
   told "with directness and power."

51 "The Pit," The Independent, LV (February 5), 331-32.
   Norris's Zolaesque purpose was to "represent human beings
   as lost in the current of some great, overpowering, brutal
   force." Norris is "notably successful" in doing this in
   The Pit, though we are left with the final impression that
   Norris has glorified "the basest passions in the American
   character." Jadwin and Crookes are drawn well, but the
   other characters are "shadowy."

52 "The Pit," Pacific Monthly, IX (June), 393.
   Norris more than equaled the "strong and rugged and true"
   story of The Octopus in The Pit. He has shown with "all the
   strength and vigor and clearness of Zola" the ignobility of
   the speculator and the evil that he does. At the same time
   he has truly illustrated the positive force of love.

53 "The Pit," Spectator, XC (February 14), 262-63.
   The Pit is without style and charm; yet it proves to be
   "a really striking novel" because of the powerful way in
   which Norris depicts "mammon worship." Norris gives us an
   excellent understanding of the motivating factors in the
   American businessman's personality.

54 "The Pit," London Times Literary Supplement (February 20), p.
   56.
   The posthumous publication of The Pit is "a mistake from
   every literary point of view." It is still in a "rough
   draft state." The wheat-pit scenes have no artistic rela-
   tion to the rest of the book; the female characters are
   for the most part lifeless. In Laura Norris has again given
   us the only kind of woman that he was capable of drawing;
   she is another Blix. The Octopus was a much better book.

55 PRESTON, HARRIET WATERS. "Lady Rose's Daughter: The Novels Of
   Mr. Norris," Atlantic Monthly, XCI (May), 691-92.
   The Octopus and The Pit are the "two most impressive and
   memorable works of fiction recently published in America."
   The Octopus is "painful to read and disquieting to remember,"
   but it is truly "a revelation, an eruption of the subliminal
   verities." Though it lacks a central plot, it "quivers with
   tragedy." In The Pit Norris fully matured. He had learned
   how to more effectively handle his narrative and give structure to his work.

56 RAINSFORD, W. S. "Frank Norris," The World's Work, V (April),
    3276.
        Norris "takes it for granted that ordinary people... are
    interesting enough to write about," and he does it without
    "a trace of the sordid." Rainsford praises Norris both as
    a writer and a man.

57 "The Rambler," The Lamp, XXVII (November), 342–44.
        Norris would never have published The Responsibilities of
    the Novelist himself. Some of the essays are "amazingly
    good," but all are "young and uneven" and not particularly
    original.

58 "The Responsibilities of the Novelist," Athenaeum (November 28),
    p. 718.
        Although Norris "exaggerates somewhat" the influence of
    the novelist upon society, The Responsibilities of the Nov-
    elist is a "readable" book, and its contents are "good and
    wholesome."

59 "The Responsibilities of the Novelist," Nation, LXXVII (November
    19), 411–12.
        While one may admire the personal ardor behind the essays,
    Norris's shrillness and smugness in The Responsibilities of
    the Novelist may put the reader off. The essays are "casual
    papers" that reveal some unfortunate defects in taste, knowl-
    edge, and judgment.

60 "The Responsibilities of the Novelist," Out West, XIX (December),
    688.
        Norris's essays are "always vigorous, often polemic, and,
    without exception, show marks of haste and lack of prepara-
    tion." The Responsibilities of the Novelist is of value
    principally because it states Norris's self-imposed standards
    as a novelist.

61 "The Responsibilities of the Novelist," Spectator, XCI (October
    31), 710.
        Anyone who wants to write a novel, from the "American
    point of view," will find The Responsibilities of the Novel-
    ist "useful."

62 "The Romance of Commerce," Academy and Literature , LXIV (Feb-
    ruary 14), 153–54.
        One would not expect to find anything romantic at the
    Chicago Board of Trade, but Norris has looked beneath the
    surface, found it, and captured it. The Pit is an exceptional
    novel because it is one "of the few that hit the balance of
    a man's life, which wavers ever between the world of action
    and the world of sentiment."

1903

63 S. D. S., Jr. "A Deal In Wheat And Other Stories," The Reader,
    II (November), 635-36.
        A Deal In Wheat is a collection of humorous, pathetic,
    and realistic stories. The best one is "A Memorandum Of
    Sudden Death," a simple but powerful setting forth of "the
    throes of death."

64 "A Significant Novel," The Outlook, LXXIII (January 17), 152-53.
        The Pit is a powerfully insightful study of American life,
    but Norris still shows signs of his immaturity. He still
    had much to learn about the subtle touches of "social por-
    traiture." Yet it is a great advance over his previous work,
    and is undoubtedly the product of a "master." Because of
    The Pit we no longer think of Norris in connection with Zola
    but with the vivid and powerful Blazac.

65 STEPHENS, HENRY MORSE. "The Work of Frank Norris: An Appreci-
    ation," The University of California Chronicle, V (January),
    324-31.
        Stephens recounts his introduction to Norris's writing in
    1899 when McTeague was being widely read and discussed by
    students at Cornell University. To Stephens, Norris's great-
    est attraction as a writer was his continually growing con-
    ception of the sphere of his art. While other regional
    writers were assuming a narrow point of view, Norris, es-
    pecially after McTeague and A Man's Woman, widened the scope
    of his vision in the manner of Zola.

66 "Stories of the East and West," Argonaut, LIII (September 26),
    325.
        A Deal in Wheat records the "eager ardor and boundless
    curiosity with which this promising young writer has turned
    his bright, investigating gaze upon the more novel phases of
    our Western life."

67 "The Story Of 'The Pit,'" London Express (March 7), p. 4.
        The "force and consequence" of The Pit mark Norris as one
    of the great descriptive writers of our time. The story it-
    self is "not remarkable," but the "surroundings" which Norris
    creates will be of great interest to Englishmen. Norris's
    analyses of Chicago life and the American businessman are
    "remarkable."

68 "A Striking Novel," Review of Reviews (English), XXVII (March),
    304.
        The Pit exhibits the power and realism seen in The Octopus,
    but Norris has now "handled his materials with greater skill."
    The opening scene of The Pit is "crude," but Norris's grasp

of his subject thereafter is undeniably great. Had Norris
lived longer, his "remarkable power and insight" would have
resulted in a very significant effect upon American literature.

69 "Tales Of Norris," New York Times: Saturday Review of Books and
    Art, LII (September 26), 652.
        A Deal in Wheat is a fine collection of "forceful, dram-
    atic, high-colored tales" done in "wonderfully enlivening
    dialect."

70 THOMPSON, FRANCIS. "The Responsibilities of the Novelist, and
    Other Literary Essays," Academy and Literature, LXV (Nov-
    ember 7), 491.
        The essays in The Responsibilities of the Novelist contain
    nothing essentially "new," but they are of interest because
    of what they reveal about Norris's attitude toward his own
    works and because of the intensely earnest tone that Norris
    takes when discussing the profession of writing.

71 "'Truth,'" Indianapolis News (February 28), p. 8.
        In opening this review of Truth, the author laments the
    deaths of Zola and Norris, two writers who shared similar
    aims and methods.

72 VAN WESTRUM, A. SCHADE. "Second Canto Of The Epic Of The Wheat,"
    The Lamp, XXVI (February), 54-56.
        After A Man's Woman Norris changed. As The Octopus il-
    lustrates, his views became broader, his insight deeper, and
    his grasp stronger. We see this again in The Pit. It pre-
    sents a forcefully told and magnificently true to life story.
    And in it we note that Norris moved past his reliance on
    Zola's style to establish his own. "Norris made an indelible
    mark upon our literature before he died."

73 WISTER, OWN. "'The Pit--A Story Of Chicago,'" The World's Work,
    V (February), 3133-34.
        The Pit was written by a master. It is a powerful, com-
    pelling tale. In dealing with the pursuit of wealth and its
    effects, Norris has "outstripped" contemporary novelists like
    Frederic, Benson, and Hope. Only in the relation of small
    talk does he falter. His death means a "great loss to our
    national literature."

1904

1904

1 SANCHEZ, NELLIE VAN DE GRIFT. "Frank Norris' Memorial Seat,"
Sunset, XII (April), 560-61.
Reports that Mrs. Robert Louis Stevenson and Gelett
Burgess designed a memorial to Norris: a stone seat near
the cabin which Norris purchased just before his untimely
death.

1905

1 The Complete Works of Frank Norris. New York: P. F. Collier
and Son, n. d.
A salesman's dummy prepared to sell the four volume
complete works. Contains summaries of Norris's six published novels, two long quotations from "Essays on Author-
ship," criticism of these essays, a review of The Pit, a
long quotation from The Pit, and forty-eight pages from The
Octopus. The thesis about Norris being emphasized is that
he was "an artist to the finger tips," whose major concern
in life was truth.

2 LEVICK, MILNE B. "Frank Norris," Overland Monthly, XLV (June),
504-08.
Levick interprets Norris as a novelist shaped by "many
masters" and by his being more concerned about forces, "the
whirl of things," than about men.

1907

1 CLIFT, DENISON HAILEY. "The Artist in Frank Norris," Pacific
Monthly, XVII (March), 313-22.
A very detailed biographical and critical essay. Clift
records the particulars of Norris's career and portrays him
as a master writer who was only entering his mature phase
at the time of his death. He reveals the literal referents
for characters and places in Norris's works.

2 "Our Own Times," The Reader, XI (May), 683-84.
An introductory comment concerning Norris's enthusiastic
membership in Phi Gamma Delta precedes the presentation of
his farcical poem, "The Exile's Toast."

1908

1 "The Spinners' Book of Fiction," Nation, LXXXVI (January 30), 107.
    The Spinners' Book is "a sheaf of fiction worth the gathering." Norris's contribution, "A Lost Story," is not mentioned.

1909

1 CORYN, SIDNEY G. P. "Books and Authors," Argonaut, LXV (September 11), 168.
    The Third Circle contains "stories that are now so well known as to need no further word of commendation." Coryn notes that three of the stories first appeared in Argonaut.

2 EDGAR, RANDOLPH. "'Studio Sketches Of A Novelist.'" The Bellman, XIII (July 17), 862.
    Each story and sketch in The Third Circle reveals "those powers of close observation and vivid rendering that made distinctive" the later works of Norris's career. The book presents "an incomparable study of the way a genius takes to find himself" during his apprenticeship.

3 "Frank Norris' 'Third Circle,'" California Weekly, I (June 25), 485.
    The Third Circle contains stories of old San Francisco "with its terrible conditions in the Chinese quarter, and the countless incidents that made thinking men and women thrill with excitement and horror." Will Irwin's introduction is summarized.

4 [GILDER, JEANETTE.] "The Lounger," Putnam's Magazine, VI (August), 629–33.
    Gilder finds that she likes Norris's short stories better than his novels. She praises Norris's descriptive ability and his power to capture "the mysterious, romantic, gruesome San Francisco" of old. San Francisco should erect a monument to Norris.

5 IRWIN, WILL. "Introduction," The Third Circle. New York: John Lane Company, pp. 7-11.
    During his career as "sub-editor" of the San Francisco Wave, Norris possessed a capacity to grow from experience, an attribute which makes his early stories especially significant when compared with his later "large and virile novels."

1909

6 "Norris, Frank," ALA Booklist, VI (October), 56.
   The stories in The Third Circle are not so good as Norris's
   mature works, but they are entertaining and show his early
   "versatility and realistic bent."

7 "Reviews," Sewanee Review, XVII (October), 501.
   Each story merits its own place in The Third Circle. The
   stories all have intrinsic value and should not be viewed
   merely as indicators of Norris's growth during his apprentice
   period.

8 SIMONDS, WILLIAM E. A Student's History of American Literature.
   Boston: Houghton Mifflin and Company, p. 353.
   Norris's uncompleted trilogy of wheat is "worthy of more
   than passing note." His accomplishment in The Octopus and
   The Pit was "remarkable."

9 "Sixteen Stories By Frank Norris: 'The Third Circle,'" San Francisco Call (June 13), p. 7.
   Praises Norris's insight into human nature as it is revealed by The Third Circle. In these stories "the primal
   instincts...of mankind, are laid bare as with a scalpel."

10 STANTON, THEODORE. A Manual of American Literature. New York:
   Putnam's, pp. 230-32.
   Had he lived, Norris would have been "equal to his task"
   of completing the wheat trilogy.

11 "Stories By Frank Norris," New York Times Review of Books, LVIII
   (May 29), 339.
   Although none of the stories in The Third Circle is of much
   importance, they all reveal Norris's powers of observation
   and his ability to vividly render the details of life. The
   volume is another reminder of how much we lost when Norris
   died.

12 "The Third Circle," The Academy, LXXVII (August 14), 419.
   The Third Circle contains "good and notable" stories.
   Not one is without interest.

13 "The Third Circle," Athenaeum (August 21), p. 206.
   Some of these early stories by Norris in The Third Circle
   are not worth preserving. They are journalistic rather than
   literary in character, but, at the same time, they do contain
   many imaginative touches.

14 "The Third Circle," The Bookman (English), XXXVII (October), 54.
        Norris's apprentice writings in The Third Circle are the
    exception to the rule: it is a collection of stories which
    deserve to be republished. There are "touches of character,
    of imaginative realism and knowledge of the underside of
    human life which are instinct with a promise that Norris had
    only half realized when his short life ended."

15 "The Third Circle," Nation, LXXXVIII (June 17), 607.
        The Third Circle contains "brilliant magazine stories,"
    but they are hardly the works of genius that Will Irwin des-
    cribes in his introduction.

16 "'The Third Circle,'", Saturday Review (English), CVIII (August
    28), 264.
        The stories in The Third Circle do not show Norris at his
    best but do contain many vivid scenes. They were "well worth
    collecting."

17 "The Third Circle," Spectator, CIII (September 18), 425.
        The sketches in The Third Circle are "unequal" in quality,
    though they are all "especially interesting." The volume is
    "well worth reading."

1910

1   SLOSSON, EDWIN E. "Great American Universities," The Independent
    LXVIII (March 3), 447-66.
        Norris consistently appeals to "book lovers in the college
    set," even though Norris's works represent a "marked devia-
    tion from the popular taste of the day." Students are attract-
    ed to Norris because of his "realism."

1911

1   COOPER, FREDERIC TABER. "Frank Norris," Some American Story
    Tellers, New York: Henry Holt and Co., pp. 295-330.
        Cooper draws extensively upon his earlier reviews and arti-
    cles concerning Norris's work. He here restates his central
    point about Norris: that Norris's chief shortcoming was his
    need to view life both realistically and romantically. Norris
    was thus frequently at odds with himself in his work. Never-
    theless, Cooper praises all of Norris's novels, especially
    McTeague and The Pit, as superb achievements.

1912

1 EAST, HARRY M. "A Lesson From Frank Norris," Overland Monthly,
LX (December), 533-34.
There are many reasons to remember Norris fondly. A
principled man, he had a sympathetic insight into human
nature that he expressed with a journalist's sense of "what
is interesting, unique, and colorful." Though some of his
work was too hastily executed, whereupon he "stuttered" and
"faltered," Norris always aimed high and continued to grow.
In The Pit and The Octopus he approached greatness.

2 "The Persisting Influence of Frank Norris," Current Literature,
LII (February), 227-28.
Largely paraphrases and quotes Cooper (1911.1). Norris
was "one of the most powerful writers America has yet produced," and one whose influence is obvious in the work of
contemporary novelists.

1913

1 DELL, FLOYD. "Chicago in Fiction: Part One," The Bookman
(American), XXXVIII (November), 270-77.
Norris believed all of the extravagant lies about Chicago
current in his day and in The Pit presented an untrue picture. Norris idyllically transformed Chicago of the 1890s.

1914

1 COOPER, FREDERIC TABER. "'Vandover And The Brute,'" The Bookman (American), XXXIX (June), 444-45.
Had Norris lived longer, he would never have made the
"colossal blunder" of publishing Vandover and the Brute in
its present form. It is powerful at points, but it is
mainly "a piece of sheer apprentice work."

2 "Current Thought In The New Books," Review of Reviews (American), XLIX (June), 761.
Vandover and the Brute is an "unusual" early work by
Norris. Its presentation of theme is crude. But, still,
it is a "very powerful" and true book.

2 "The Degradation Of A Soul," The Independent, LXXIX (August 3),
173.
Vandover and the Brute is "crude and unfinished" in
spots, yet it bears the mark of Norris's genius.

4   "Derelict By Destiny," Pall Mall Gazette (June 16), p. 9.
         Vandover and the Brute does not satisfy our expectations
     of the author of The Octopus, The Pit, and the masterpiece,
     McTeague. The stage-by-stage portrayal of Vandover's de-
     generation is tedious; moreover, "Predestination is as false
     in fiction as in theology."

5   E. F. E. [EDWIN FRANCIS EDGETT.] "Norris's Posthumous Novel,"
     Boston Evening Transcript (April 22), pt. 2, p. 8.
         Apologies for the unfinished state of Vandover and the
     Brute are unnecessary. While it might have been "more co-
     herent and compact if its writer had lived to revise it,"
     its extraordinarily vivid scenes and events reveal Norris's
     "consummate skill" as a writer. The novel proves Norris's
     "genius." Even in its unrevised form, the "forceful and
     truthful" story is superior to similar tales such as Max-
     well's In Cotton Wool and Dreiser's Sister Carrie.

6   "Frank Norris's Werewolf," Current Opinion, LVI (June), 455-56.
         Norris was a "pioneer of American ultra-realists" and
     Vandover and the Brute will be of interest to those concerned
     with the "history of English realism" and "the career of its
     brilliant and ill-starred author."

7   "In Memoriam," The University of California Chronicle, XVI (Oc-
     tober), 453.
         Relates that a memorial chair, inscribed to Norris, has
     been erected in Berkeley's Greek Theatre by a group of
     Norris's classmates.

8   MARKHAM, EDWIN. California the Wonderful. New York: Hearst,
     p. 217, 298, and 363.
         "Frank Norris stands at the forefront of Californian novel-
     ists." While McTeague and Vandover and the Brute are "mast-
     erly," his greatest work is the uncompleted trilogy of the
     wheat.

9   "Memories of Frank Norris," The Bookman (American), XXXIX (May),
     236-38.
         Summary of Norris's life, based upon Charles Norris's
     promotional pamphlet for Vandover and the Brute (1914.12).

10 "New Books and Reprints," London Times Literary Supplement (June
     18), p. 299.
         Vandover and the Brute was written when Norris, the author
     of The Octopus and The Pit, was "under the influence of
     Zolaesque pessimism."

1914

11 NORRIS, CHARLES G. "Forward," Vandover and the Brute, by Frank
      Norris. Garden City, New York: Doubleday, Page, and Co.,
      pp. v-ix.
         Tells the story of the recovery of the lost Vandover and
      the Brute manuscript and comments upon its unfinished state.

12 NORRIS, CHARLES G. The Story of the Loss and Recovery of the
      Manuscript of a Posthumous Novel by Frank Norris. Garden
      City, New York: Doubleday, Page and Co.
         Promotional pamphlet for Vandover and the Brute containing
      excerpts from Charles Norris's "Forward" (1914.11).

13 "Novel By Frank Norris," New York Times Review of Books, LXIII
      (April 12), 181-82.
         Vandover and the Brute reads as though it was Norris's
      first draft. Yet, even unrevised, it is a remarkable book
      because it is so revelatory of "the fundamental things in
      human nature."

14 "Novels Of The Season," The Literary Digest, XLVIII (June 20),
      1494-95.
         Although Vandover and the Brute exhibits the "unpruned
      crudities" of a novel lacking final revision, many "would
      gladly have a claim to its authorship." Characters are
      "elaborately introduced" and then disappear, and the "love
      element" is only sketchily drawn, but still the novel has
      "gripping force."

15 "A Posthumous Story by Frank Norris," Current Opinion, LVI (June)
      455.
         The theme of Vandover and the Brute is "that of a new
      Jekyll and Hyde, worked out in a very original way."

16 "Recent Reflections Of A Novel-Reader," Atlantic Monthly, CXIV
      (October), 525-26.
         Vandover and the Brute is "little more than a medico-
      moral treatise of the school of Brieux." This "mediocre"
      book is interesting only in that it shows "the writer's
      bent from the beginning."

17 S. '03. "Frank Norris: A Lasting Influence In Our Campus Life,"
      The California Alumni Weekly, VI (January 17), 1, 3.
         A plea for the recognition of Norris's greatness as a
      writer and as a man.

18 STEPHENS, HENRY MORSE. "An Old Novel by Frank Norris Comes to
      Light," The California Alumni Weekly, VI (April 18), 1-2.
         While Vandover and the Brute is inferior to McTeague, the
      same stylistic power is evident, especially during the scene

describing the wreck of the Mazatlan. Norris's vivid portrait of "the degeneration of a soul" has never been equaled
in fiction.

19 "A Study in Temperament," Illustrated London News, LV (July 4),
    28.
        In Vandover and the Brute Norris paints a "terrible pic-
    ture" of a man destroyed by the brute within him. "That the
    book is sincere, justifies scenes which are little less than
    emotional orgy; though there are passages of beauty and
    pathos."

20 UNDERWOOD, JOHN CURTIS. Literature and Insurgency. New York:
    Kennerly, pp. 130-78.
        The "work of Frank Norris is durable because it deals
    with the material of our common national life...his express-
    ion is permanent because it is the expression of truth it-
    self." The Octopus is certainly the greatest work produced
    in the twentieth century. Together with his other novels,
    especially McTeague, it earns Norris a high place in American
    literature. "As a product of more modern and, in many ways,
    more reactionary conditions, and as a progressive optimist
    to his last day and hour, Frank Norris deserves to be ranked
    slightly higher in the human scale than Mark Twain; and it is
    quite possible that in the long run his work will be remem-
    bered longer." Always a novelist of the "People," Norris
    sought only to be sincere, to tell the truth about real life.

21 "Vandover and the Brute," The Academy, LXXXVII (July 4), 17.
        Vandover and the Brute is "rude" and not to be compared
    with The Pit. But it is a "powerful" story, and reads like
    a translation of one of Zola's works.

22 "Vandover and the Brute," Athenaeum (June 27), p. 886.
        Vandover and the Brute would have been a much better work
    if Norris had lived to revise it, especially to eliminate
    the repetitious and unnecessarily unsavory elements. It
    is a very frank book, and perhaps a bowdlerized version
    should have been issued to the public.

23 "Vandover and the Brute," Nation, XCVIII (April 16), 432-33.
        Vandover and the Brute is a very imaginative but immature
    and rough work. Yet, while it is flawed, its "unflinching
    moral conviction...lifts it to a place not far below 'Mc-
    Teague' as a powerful private study."

1914

24 "Vandover and the Brute," The Outlook, CVII (May 30), 264-65.
    Vandover and the Brute is a remarkable pice of work for
    a young man, written with "terrible precision" in the style
    of "unadulterated realism." Zolaesque in the extreme, it
    presents a "repulsive, shocking spectacle." Reading it is
    like watching a body disintegrate.

25 "'Vandover and the Brute,'" Saturday Review (English), CXVII
    (June 20), 805.
    Vandover and the Brute is a "precocious," slavishly Zola-
    esque early work of Norris. Its characterizations, handling
    of dialogue, and "vivid" writing are good, but its crudity in
    style and conception will disappoint those who are familiar
    with Norris's finished works like The Octopus and The Pit.
    The greatest flaw is that Vandover "never strikes us as real."
    He is too much of a puppet.

26 "'Vandover and the Brute,'" London Times Literary Supplement
    (June 25), p. 311.
    Vandover and the Brute presents a strong story of a
    "terribly lonely, secret tragedy" of degeneration. Its
    realism is Zolaesque, but it does not offend because of
    Norris's obvious sincerity in handling the subject.

1915

1 ELDREDGE, ZOETH SKINNER. History of California. New York: The
    Century Publishing Company, pp. 498-99.
    Norris's unfinished Wheat trilogy captures the spirit of
    "adventurous daring which marked the early pioneers" of Cal-
    ifornia, though his earlier work demonstrates more artistry.

2 KELLNER, LEON. American Literature, trans. Julia Franklin,
    Garden City, New York: Doubleday, Page and Co., pp. 23-24.
    Translation of volume by Kellner cited in "Works In
    Foreign Languages." Reference to Norris as a significant
    American realistic writer.

3 PATTEE, FRED LEWIS. A History of American Literature since 1870.
    New York: The Century Co., pp. 398-400.
    The Octopus and The Pit are impressive in scope. McTeague
    and Vandover and the Brute are brutal in theme. In different
    ways all the novels show that Norris "unquestionably lacked

1917

knowledge of many of the most fundamental areas of human life
...Like the mere journalists, he was obsessed with...the value
of the present moment. He lacked a sense of the past...he
lacked the elements that make for the literature of performance."

4 [SLOSSON, EDWIN E.] "Literature, American and English", The
     International Year Book: 1914. New York: Dodd, Mead &
     Company, p. 417.
        Vandover and the Brute "depicts the degeneration of a
     soul."

1916

1 EDGAR, RANDOLPH. "The Manuscript and the Man," The Bellman, XX
     (May 27, 1916), 602-03.
        In 1914, Edgar received 14 pages and fragments of the
     McTeague manuscript from Charles G. Norris. This portion of
     manuscript, as he received it, represented a printer's "take"
     for the first impression of the novel, corresponding to about
     twenty pages of printed text.

2 HATHORN, RALPH. "The Origin of the Pig Dinner," Phi Gamma Delta
     Quarterly, XXXVIII (February), 424-27.
        A detailed account of the first Phi Gamma Delta "pig
     dinner," at which Norris served as the "High Priest."

1917

1 MENCKEN, HENRY LOUIS. A Book of Prefaces. New York: Alfred A.
     Knopf, pp. 70-71, passim.
        Drieser's Sister Carrie owes no literary debt to Norris.
     Dreiser was a bigger man and a better novelist than Norris.

2 WYATT, EDITH. "Vandover and the Brute," Great Companions. New
     York: Appleton Co., pp. 48-58.
        Norris's best qualities as a novelist--his "power of hon-
     esty," his sincerity, his handling of setting and ability to

1917

improvise--make <u>Vandover and the Brute</u> a better book than those in the Wheat trilogy. <u>Vandover and the Brute</u> is as good a novel as <u>McTeague</u>.

1918

1   PANCOAST, HENRY S. "Introduction," <u>McTeague</u>, by Frank Norris. New York: Boni and Liveright.
     Norris's own experiences and observations of everyday life animated his novels in a remarkable manner. He worked with the commonplace in <u>McTeague</u>, and at the same time he transcended the restrictions of time and place to depict all of the ugliness and crudity of Western civilization.

2   WILLIAMS, HAROLD H. <u>Modern English Writers</u>. London: Sidgwick & Jackson, Limited, pp. 457, 473-75.
     Like Zola, Norris believed that the story of a novel should enforce its theme. Norris successfully concerned himself with "big" ideas in his works. His works are marred only by his stylistic techniques.

1919

1   BOYNTON, PERCY H. <u>A History of American Literature</u>. Boston: Ginn and Company, p. 432.
     Few novelists of social criticism in the late nineteenth century equalled the quality of Norris's writing in books such as <u>The Octopus</u>, <u>The Pit</u>, and <u>Vandover and the Brute</u>. Norris's "breadth of vision" distinguished him as superior to the "muckraker" writers.

1920

1   MARCOSSON, ISAAC F. <u>Adventures in Interviewing</u>. New York: John Lane Co., pp. 36-37, 78, 232-41, 255, 272, 273, 276, 280, 288.
     Marcosson reconstructs his literary and personal friendship with Norris, presenting several letters he received from Norris. Marcosson believes that Norris had definitely "arrived" by the time of his death, and that Norris "might have produced a piece of work vitally and permanently American" if he had lived longer.

2   SANCHEZ, NELLIE VAN DE GRIFT. The Life of Mrs. Robert Louis
    Stevenson. New York: Charles Scribner's Sons, pp. 275-78.
       Briefly describes Norris's friendly relationship with
    Mrs. Stevenson and his plans to build a summer house near the
    Stevenson ranch. Relates that Norris and Mrs. Stevenson "were
    persuaded to record their voices in a phonograph."

                              1921

1   TRENT, WILLIAM PETERFIELD, et al., eds. The Cambridge History of
    American Literature, III. New York: Putnam's, pp. 93-94.
       Norris "had larger aims than Crane and on the whole
    achieved more"; his lack of sectionalism, even in the "Califor-
    nia" novels, demonstrates his youthful vigor and concern for
    "truth" in fiction.

                              1922

1   GARNETT, EDWARD. Friday Nights. New York: Alfred A. Knopf,
    pp. 295-96.
       Norris's "psychological force and nervous creative inten-
    sity" permit instant and total acquaintance with the charac-
    ters of The Octopus.

2   HALL, ERNEST JACKSON. The Satirical Element in the American
    Novel. Philadelphia: University of Pennsylvania Press,
    p. 39.
       The Octopus and The Pit border on satire of political and
    economic conditions, but are "too realistic to be truly sa-
    tirical."

3   RANKIN, T. E. and W. M. AIKIN. American Literature. New York:
    Harcourt, Brace, and Co., pp. 257-59.
       Norris exhibits the influence of Stevenson in Moran of
    the Lady Letty and Zola in McTeague, but he saw himself as
    neither a romantic nor a realist. His aim was to express
    "the significance of the real" in his own fashion; and his
    craftmanship has influenced a great many artists. The Oc-
    topus was not the great American novel, yet it was a "land-
    mark...on the way to that yearned for achievement." McTeague
    is "repulsively realistic," and The Pit is inferior to The
    Octopus.

1923

1   EDGAR, RANDOLPH, comp. "Frank Benjamin Franklin Norris, 1870-
    1902," Publishers' Weekly, CIII (March 3), 637.
        Brief primary bibliography of Norris's works appearing in
    "book form" to 1922.

2   HANEY, JOHN LOUIS. The Story of Our Literature: An Interpre-
    tation of the American Spirit. New York: Scribner's p. 257.
        "After writing several novels that attracted little atten-
    tion, he conceived a trilogy of stories comprising "the Epic
    of Wheat," in which he preached social democracy.

3   "New Novels", London Times Literary Supplement, CXV (May 31),
    370.
        The Third Circle contains "vigorous" but often "immature"
    pieces of magazine fiction.

4   PATTEE, FRED LEWIS. The Development of the American Short Story.
    New York: Harper, pp. 337-39, passim.
        Norris was a novelist primarily. He believed the short
    story to be an "ephemeral" genre, not worth care or pain.
    "Perhaps no other American novelist has been so little en-
    dowed by nature for working with the short story form."

1924

1   FIRKINS, OSCAR W. William Dean Howells: A Study. Cambridge:
    Harvard University Press, p. 160.
        A single reference to the character of Jadwin in The Pit.

2   "From Section Hand to 'Movie' Star," Southern Pacific Bulletin,
    XIII (March), 17.
        The 34th Street Station in Oakland, California, was the
    exact location of McTeague's proposal to Trina in McTeague
    and was the setting for the corresponding episode in Erich
    Von Stroheim's film Greed, adapted from the novel.

1925

1   KNIGHT, GRANT C. Superlatives. New York: Alfred A. Knopf,
    pp. 118-38.
        Vanamee in The Octopus is the "greatest lover" in English
    and American fiction. Norris could write the sensuous and
    lyrical story of Vanamee and his search for Angele in a
    novel such as The Octopus because "his theory of novel
    writing permitted him to make his realism attractive rather
    than ugly."

1926

2 NORRIS, KATHLEEN. "Introduction," Blix. Garden City: Doubleday, Page, and Co., pp. vii-viii.
        In Blix, more than in any other of his novels, Norris re-
   lates the "story of his early youth."

3 SINCLAIR, UPTON. "The California Octopus," Mammonart: An Essay
   in Economic Interpretation. Pasadena: The Author, pp. 349-
   52.
        Sinclair praises Norris for describing urban ills with
   Zolaesque realism in McTeague. He relates that the exposé
   of The Octopus startled him as a young man; it first opened
   his eyes to the corruption of trusts in America. He finds
   that Norris's moral credo as an artist, expressed in The
   Responsibilities of the Novelist, was exactly the same as
   his own. In closing, he laments Norris's lapse from his high
   moral purpose when he wrote The Pit, a comparatively "tame
   and conventional" novel.

4 VAN DOREN, CARL AND MARK VAN DOREN. American and British Literature Since 1890. New York: The Century Company, pp. 48-50,
   passim.
        Norris had "more force than direction." He was heavy
   handed and repetitive. The Octopus is his major work.

1926

1 BEER, THOMAS. The Mauve Decade. New York: Alfred A. Knopf,
   passim.
        Norris depicted the "relentless sense of human movement"
   in his writings. In The Octopus and The Pit his moralistic
   tendencies came to dominate his style in a melodramatic
   fashion. (For a response, see Meyer [1943.2].)

2 CHAMBERLIN, WILLIAM FOSDICK. The History of Phi Gamma Delta.
   New York: The Fraternity of Phi Gamma Delta, pp. 118-26,
   411.
        In 1893, Norris originated the fraternity's annual "pig
   dinner," which was known after his death as the "Norris
   Dinner." Norris's poem, "The Exile's Toast," reprinted
   here, was read at the dinner held in 1900.

3 DONDORE, DOROTHY ANNE. The Prairie and the Making of Middle
   America: Four Centuries of Description. Cedar Rapids, Iowa:
   Torch Press, pp. 337-40.
        In The Pit Norris places an individual against nature it-
   self, making Jadwin the "logical successor to the pioneer."

1926

4   MENCKEN, H. L. Prejudices: Fifth Series. New York: Alfred A.
       Knopf, p. 232.
          Had Norris lived, he might have written a satire of the
       "American Puritan," for, despite his romantic and mystical
       proclivities, Norris was first a satirist.

5   MUMFORD, LEWIS. The Golden Day: A Study in American Literature
       and Culture. New York: Boni & Liveright, Inc., pp. 240-41.
          In The Pit and The Octopus Norris "faced the brutal in-
       dustrialism" of turn-of-the-century America.

1927

1   CALVERTON, VICTOR FRANCIS. The Liberation of American Literature.
       New York: Charles Scribner's Sons, pp. 350-54, passim.
          Norris, America's first "determinist," sounds the beginning
       of the "defeatist mood" in American literature. Yet even he
       sidestepped the issues posed by sex.

2   HAZARD, LUCY LOCKWOOD. The Frontier in American Literature. New
       York: Thomas Y. Crowell Company, pp. 267-70, passim.
          The Octopus chronicles the passing of the frontier and
       the death of the agricultural phase of American culture.

1928

1   CHISLETT, WILLIAM. Moderns and Near Moderns. New York: Graf-
       ton Press, pp. 109-11, 116-20.
          Norris's critical essays disclose that he actually ap-
       plied the techniques of writing a short story to the compos-
       ing of a novel. This fact combined with his journalistic
       exuberance produced novels for "the young."

2   COBB, IRVIN S. "Foreword," The Argonaut Manuscript Limited E-
       dition of Frank Norris' Works, I. Garden City: Doubleday,
       Doran & Company, pp. ix-x.
          Norris was a "pioneer of the modern school of native
       realists' who managed to differentiate between "realism"
       and "dullness."

3   DOBIE, CHARLES CALDWELL. "Frank Norris, or, Up from Culture,"
    American Mercury, XIII (April), 412-424.
        Stressing the over-powering effect of "romance" on Norris,
    Dobie presents a narrative of Norris's childhood, his antece-
    dents, his literary influences, and his novelistic career,
    concluding with a short analysis of the major novels.

4   ____. "Introduction," The Argonaut Manuscript Limited Edition
    of Frank Norris' Works, VIII. Garden City: Doubleday,
    Doran & Company, pp. v-xxxii.
        Reprinted from 1928.3

5   DREISER, THEODORE. "Introduction," The Argonaut Manuscript
    Limited Edition of Frank Norris' Works, VIII. Garden City:
    Doubleday, Doran & Company, pp. vii-xi.
        Norris was a "pioneer realist," preceded only by Fuller
    and far more important than Crane. McTeague is simply the
    best realistic work of all time.

6   HOWELLS, MILDRED, ed. Life in Letters of William Dean Howells,
    II. Garden City: Doubleday, Doran & Company, p. 102.
        Howells informs Harper & Brothers on March 4, 1899 that
    he intends to "get a topic out of Norris's McTeague" for an
    essay.

7   HUGHES, RUPERT. "Introduction," The Argonaut Manuscript Limited
    Edition of Frank Norris' Works, III. Garden City: Double-
    day, Doran & Company, pp. ix-xiii.
        Moran of the Lady Letty is closely akin to Medea in that
    both tell of an "uncouth but magnificent barbarian."

8   IRWIN, WILL. "Introduction," The Argonaut Manuscript Limited
    Edition of Frank Norris' Works, IV. Garden City: Double-
    day, Doran & Company, pp. vii-ix.
        Reprinted from 1909.5.

9   MARBLE, ANNIE RUSSELL. A Study of the Modern Novel: British
    and American, Since 1900. New York, London: D. Appleton
    and Co., pp. 364, 366, 367.
        The Pit "exposed the deals and corruption of the wheat
    market," and apparently influenced both Herrick's The Common
    Lot and Dreiser's The Titan.

10 MENCKEN, H. L. "Introduction," The Argonaut Manuscript Limited
    Edition of Frank Norris' Works, V. Garden City: Doubleday,
    Doran & Company, pp. ix-x.
        Using Charles Norris's account as a point of departure,
    Mencken briefly retells the tortuous story of the publica-

tion of Vandover and the Brute. The novel has a "genuine
dramatic power." The influence of Zola is fortunate, for
Vandover and the Brute is less "sleek" than The Pit.

11 MORLEY, CHRISTOPHER. "Foreword," The Argonaut Manuscript Limited Edition of Frank Norris' Works, VI. Garden City,
Doubleday, Doran & Company, pp. ix-x.
"It is the curious anomaly of a wood-pulp plot married to
an executive skill of the first order, that makes [A Man's
Woman] so queer a study," for Norris deftly combines melodramatic hyperbole with "savory technical detail" in this
novel.

12 NORRIS, CHARLES G. "Introduction," The Argonaut Manuscript
Limited Edition of Frank Norris' Works, X. Garden City:
Doubleday, Doran & Company, pp. vii-xiii.
Norris progressed steadily from a crude, unpolished writer
to a successful, deliberate novelist.

13 NORRIS, KATHLEEN. "Introduction," The Argonaut Manuscript Lim-
ited Edition of Frank Norris' Works, III. Garden City:
Doubleday, Doran & Company, pp. vii-viii.
Reprinted from 1925.2.

14 OVERTON, GRANT. "Foreword," The Argonaut Manuscript Limited
Edition of Frank Norris' Works, VII. Garden City: Doubleday, Doran & Company, pp. xxxiii-xii.
The essays in The Responsibilities of the Novelist may
be divided into two categories: those which treat the
business of publishing and those which deal with Norris's
theory of fiction, the contemporary literary scene, and the
business of writing. But the judgments, criticisms, obser-
vations, and predictions Norris makes in any of the essays
still hold.

15 PARRINGTON, VERNON LOUIS. "The Development of Realism," in Norman Foerster, ed., The Reinterpretation of American Literature. New York: Harcourt, Brace, and Co., pp. 143, 154-155.
Norris is co-creator with Crane of the uniquely American
brand of realism, that is, naturalism.

16 TOMPKINS, JULIET WILBOR. "Introduction," The Argonaut Manuscript
Limited Edition of Frank Norris' Works, IX. Garden City:
Doubleday, Doran & Company, pp. vii-x.
Norris's brief but happy days with his wife Jeannette in
New York were characterized by boyishness, bouyancy, robust-
ness, charm, and a delight in games.

1929

1 GRATTAN, C. HARTLEY. <u>Bitter Bierce</u>: <u>A Mystery of American</u>
<u>Letters</u>. Garden City: Doubleday, Doran & Co., pp. 3, 273.
  Norris in contradistinction to Bierce eventually surrendered his position as a critic of his social environment by
succumbing to that environment.

2 ———. "Frank Norris," <u>Bookman</u> (American), LXIX (July 10),
506-10.
  Lacking the ability to deal with ideas, Norris's literary
"rebellion" was "emotional and disorderly." This is especially evident in his essays, and it may also be seen in his
fiction. Norris saw fiction as simply another form of jour-
nalism, a matter of reporting, and he was more concerned
with capturing facts than with his manner of expressing them.
Yet, despite this, he managed to write three great books:
<u>McTeague</u>, <u>Vandover and the Brute</u>, and <u>The Octopus</u>.

3 LEISY, ERNEST ERWIN. <u>American Literature</u>: <u>An Interpretative</u>
<u>Survey</u>. New York: Thomas Y. Crowell Company, pp. 207-08.
  Norris "sought in all his writing, whether it dealt with
farming, or shark-fishing, or the bohemian life delineated
in his less-known books, to portray with undevidating hon-
esty the elemental facts concerning human nature."

4 OVERTON, GRANT M. <u>An Hour of the American Novel</u>. Philadelphia,
London: J. B. Lippincott Co., pp. 109-11.
  After succumbing to the influence of Kipling and Zola,
Norris produced <u>The Octopus</u> and <u>The Pit</u>, "novels of high
order," on which his reputation stands. Seldom has a novel-
ist written with such firm control and power.

5 VAN DOREN, CARL. "Frank Norris" in Cunliffe, Marcus, ed., <u>The</u>
<u>Columbia University Course in Literature</u>, XVIII. New York:
Columbia University Press, pp. 481-83.
  Since Norris's life was cut short, "he must remain notable not for the depth which age might have brought but the
fire and strength which he had from his youth." Although
his heroes and heroines are almost all of a type, his subject matter breathes originality.

1930

1 COTTRELL, GEORGE W. AND HOXIE N. FAIRCHILD. <u>Critical Guide</u>:
<u>Prepared for the Home Study Course in World Literature,</u>
<u>based on the Columbia University Course in Literature</u>, pub-
<u>lished by the Columbia University Press</u>. New York: Columbia

1930

University Press, p. 377.
   The Octopus combines French naturalism with pure sentiment.

2   EDGAR, RANDOLPH. "The Revival of Frank Norris," Boston Evening
      Transcript (May 3), pp. 1-2.
         The publication of new editions of The Octopus and The Pit
      may create a new interest in Norris.

3   EVERETT, WALLACE W. "Frank Norris in His Chapter," The Phi Gamma
      Delta Quarterly, LII (April), 561-66.
         A biographical sketch of Norris as the "paragon of a true
      fraternity man;" relates his activities and describes his
      popular image at Berkeley during his college years.

4   FOERSTER, NORMAN. Toward Standards: A Study of the Present
      Critical Movement in American Letters. New York: Farrar
      and Rinehart, Inc., p. 137.
         Passing reference to Norris as one of several authors of
      the "nineties" through whose work realism was announced.

5   HOWARD, ERIC. "Frank Norris" in Rockwell D. Hunt, ed., California
      and Californians, IV. Chicago and New York: Lewis Publish-
      ing Company, pp. 89-90.
         Norris "saw life clearly and wrote of it as it is, with
      a realistic power that has seldom been equaled in American
      literature. His work is broad in conception, thorough in
      execution and elemental in appeal." His greatest work is
      McTeague which attracted the attention of the public because
      it dealt with a level of life new to American fiction.

6   LEWIS, OSCAR. "Frank Norris' California Locale," Hesperian
      (Winter), unpaged.
         Unlike many so-called California writers, who used Cal-
      ifornia merely as a setting, Norris distilled the essence of
      California, especially of San Francisco, into his best work,
      thoroughly fusing setting to his themes, characters, and
      other aspects of his novels.

7   O'DELL, BARRY. "Recollecting Frank Norris," San Franciscan, V
      (December), 12, 36.
         With Zola, Stevenson, and Kipling as his models, Norris
      produced in McTeague the best picture of San Francisco ever
      executed. But his own best book was The Octopus, a "magni-
      ficent illustration of the power which economic machinery has
      over the primary elements of life."

1931

8 PARRINGTON, VERNON LOUIS. Main Currents in American Thought,
      III. New York: Harcourt, Brace, & World, Inc., pp. 329-34,
      passim.
         Heavily influenced by Zola, Norris "began as a romantic
      and worked out of it slowly," though he never captured the
      completely amoral attitude which his literary essays rec-
      ommend for the writer of fiction. (For responses, see Meyer,
      1943.2 and Pizer, 1955.5.)

9 PATTEE, FRED LEWIS. The New American Literature, 1890-1930.
      New York: Century, pp. 36-48, passim. As a writer, Norris
      attempted to give his readers "Truth." Rebelling against
      the conventions of his period, he produced stories and nov-
      els written with an eye which was "telescopic, not micro-
      scopic like the local colorists." Yet, despite his fervor,
      his later work exhibits "symptoms of surrender" to the very
      conventions he hated. Even so, McTeague and The Octopus
      deserve places on "the short shelf of American 'classics.'"

10 TAYLOR, HARVEY. Frank Norris: Two Poems and "Kim" Reviewed.
      San Francisco: Harvey Taylor, unpaged.
         Contains a six page bibliography of "The First Editions
      of Frank Norris," which Charles G. Norris called "the best
      bibliography of my brother's writings that has been made."
      (In a letter appearing in the volume.)

11 WAGENKNECHT, EDWARD. "Frank Norris in Retrospect," Virginia
      Quarterly Review, VI (April), 313-20.
         Norris possessed a number of traits "that many of our
      novelists today seem to lack:" a quality of genius, an
      ability to fuse romance and realism, a knack for unusual de-
      tail, and a recognition of the necessity of personal integ-
      rity.

                        1931

1 BOYNTON, PERCY H. The Rediscovery of the Frontier. Chicago:
      University of Chicago Press, pp. 77-79, 85.
         Norris's "stories of the wheat are the combinations of
      hard fact and sentimental optimism that one becomes used
      to in the fiction of the frontier."

2 BRITTEN, FLORENCE HAXTON. "'Prissy' Frank Norris," New York
      Herald Tribune Books (August 23), p. 13.
         There is nothing special about the early newspaper pieces
      collected in Frank Norris of "The Wave." Norris's better
      early work was included in The Third Circle. The most inter-
      esting thing illustrated by the present volume is how much
      of a prig Norris was.

1931

3   CHAMBERLAIN, J. "The 'Prentice Days of Frank Norris," New York
    Times Book Review, LXXX (May 2), 2, 10.
        The sketches in Frank Norris of "The Wave" vary in excel-
    lence. They are most valuable because of the light they cast
    on the many facets of young Norris's personality. They are
    also of interest because many of them anticipate later de-
    velopments in Norris's novels.

4   DEMILLE, GEORGE E. Literary Criticism in America: A Preliminary
    Survey. New York: L. MacVeagh, The Dial Press, pp. 194,
    198-202.
        Norris was "potentially a great critic"; his literary
    criticism has not received the attention it deserves. His
    defense of novelists and novel-writing carries a note of
    "evangelical seriousness" which makes his single volume of
    critical essays especially important for students of the
    genre.

5   DOBIE, CHARLES CALDWELL. "The First Californian Authors," The
    Bookman (American), LXXII (February), 590-96.
        Though not a native of the state, Norris succeeded very
    well in interpreting different aspects of life in California.
    None of his works is as strong, however, as McTeague, the
    novel he composed first.

6   ____. "Literature on the Pacific Coast," in John Albert Macy,
    ed., American Writers on American Literature. New York:
    H. Liveright, pp. 419-20, passim.
        Norris was one of California's finest writers. His real-
    istic McTeague was his masterpiece.

7   DREISER, THEODORE. "The Early Adventures of Sister Carrie,"
    Colophon (February), [19-22].
        Norris first championed the unpublished Sister Carrie in
    his capacity of reader for Doubleday, Page, and Co.; later,
    he acted as informal advisor to Dreiser regarding his right
    to publication; and finally, he clandestinely distributed
    copies of the novel to selected reviewers.

8   GARLAND, HAMLIN. Companions on the Trail: A Literary Chronicle.
    New York: The MacMillan Company, pp. 166-71.
        Reprints Garland's tribute to Norris in The Critic (see
    1903.29), and concludes: "I feel no inclination to change
    the broad outlines of this estimate now, thirty years later."

9   GRATTAN, C. HARTLEY. "Frank Norris of 'The Wave ,'" American
    Literature, III (November), 349-50.
        Frank Norris of "The Wave" reveals that Norris's early
    journalism "was no better and no worse" than that of other

talented journalists. It leaves the impression that Norris
was "thoroughly confused" and "decidedly an intellectual
'light weight.'"

10 KNIGHT, GRANT C. The Novel in English. New York: Richard C.
    Smith, Inc., pp. 298-303.
        Norris's fame will rest on The Octopus and The Pit solely.

11 LEWIS, OSCAR. "Introduction," Frank Norris of "The Wave":
    Stories and Sketches from the San Francisco Weekly, 1893 to
    1897. San Francisco: The Westgate Press, pp. 1-15.
        Norris engaged in a "particularly realistic type of re-
    porting," and he characteristically imbued his articles with
    "lively interest and importance." In his fictional writing
    he molded his own distinctive style through experimentation.
    Blix depicts Norris during his days on the Wave.

12 MARKHAM, EDWIN. Songs and Stories. San Francisco: Powell,
    pp. 15-16.
        A recapitulation of his earlier statement in California
    the Wonderful; see 1914.8.

13 NORRIS, CHARLES G. "Foreword," Frank Norris of "The Wave":
    Stories and Sketches from the San Francisco Weekly, 1893-
    1897. San Francisco: The Westgate Press, pp. iii-v.
        The writings in this anthology represent Norris's work
    "during his most formative years." In 1896-98 Norris had
    "more certainty of purpose than at any other period in his
    life"--though he never took himself or his work too serious-
    ly. Norris's realism at this stage of his career was not
    well-received, and his father was especially disappointed
    in his work.

14 WALKER, FRANKLIN D. "Frank Norris at the University of Calif-
    ornia," University of California Chronicle, XXXIII (July),
    320-49.
        The impression Norris made upon his classmates at Berke-
    ley was that of a mature but fun-loving young man. Norris's
    distaste for the academic regimen, his positive response to
    Joseph Le Conte, and his activities in his fraternity are
    related in detail. His writings as a student are listed
    and discussed in light of his later works; and his novels
    are discussed in light of his college experience.

1932

1   BEACH, JOSEPH WARREN. The Twentieth Century Novel. New York:
      Appleton-Century-Crofts, p. 322.
         The Octopus and The Pit are "brave" attempts at realism.
      But, unlike Dreiser in his treatments of business life,
      Norris reveals too many genteel self-restraints.

2   BROOKS, VAN WYCK. Sketches in Criticism. New York: E. P.
      Dutton, pp. 173-74.
         Both The Octopus and The Pit illustrate the commonplace,
      but bewildering, fact that powerful men are often controlled
      by that which they seek to control.

3   CHAMBERLAIN, JOHN. Farewell to Reform: The Rise, Life, and
      Decay of the Progressive Mind in America. New York: Live-
      right, pp. 104-10. (Second Ed., Gloucester, Massachusetts:
      Peter Smith, 1958, pp. 104-10, passim.)
         Norris believed that chance ruled the lives of individ-
      uals, that only "the cosmic" remained eternal. In McTeague
      he writes a "study of blind determinism," while The Octopus,
      despite its confused ending, represents America's "finest
      collective work of fiction." (For a response, see Meyer,
      1943.2.)

4   DICKINSON, THOMAS H. The Making of American Literature. New
      York: Century, pp. 645-46.
         The Octopus and The Pit surpass Norris's earlier works
      in conception and art. In them he uses his sense of social
      indignation to good effect.

5   DREISER, THEODORE. "The Great American Novel," The American
      Spectator, I (December), 1-2.
         McTeague is "as fine an illustration of what American
      realism might be as America offers." Had Norris lived,
      he would have been expected to continue in the realistic
      tradition begun by Hawthorne and Melville.

6   FULLERTON, B. M. A Selective Bibliography of American Liter-
      ature, 1775-1900. New York: W. F. Payson, p. 206.
         Includes only Moran of the Lady Letty and McTeague as
      being "representative" of Norris at his best.

7   KNIGHT, GRANT C. American Literature and Culture. New York:
      Ray Long and Richard R. Smith, Inc., pp. 389-95, passim.
         The influence of Zola is present in all of Norris's work
      from his early "red-blooded" novels to his vast canvasses
      of American civilization. Norris was by no means a great
      novelist, but he greatly influenced later writers such as
      Dreiser.

1933

8   LEWISOHN, LUDWIG. Expression in America. New York: Harper &
    Brothers, passim.
        Norris was a transitional figure in the history of Amer-
    ican literature. In works such as McTeague he broke with
    the genteel tradition and helped initiate the major literary
    developments of the twentieth century.

9   WARD, ALFRED C. American Literature 1880-1930. London: Meth-
    uen and Company, Ltd., pp. 87-90.
        If Norris had controlled his journalistic "temptation to
    make his novels glorified newspapers," he could have been a
    great novelist; even with its melodrama and incoherency,
    The Octopus relates a powerful story.

10 WALKER, FRANKLIN. Frank Norris: A Biography. Garden City:
    Doubleday, Doran & Co. (Reissued, New York: Russell &
    Russell, 1963.)
        Walker pictures Norris as essentially boyish in spirit;
    he had a flair for writing which he indulged first in Paris,
    where he studied art, next at the University of California
    at Berkeley, where he enrolled as a full-time student, next
    at Harvard, where he devoted himself exclusively to writing,
    and finally in San Francisco and New York, where he launched
    his career as a professional writer. This biography is the
    first and, at present, only full-scale one of Norris.

1933

1   BOAS, RALPH PHILIP AND KATHERINE BURTON. Social Backgrounds of
    American Literature. Boston: Little, Brown, and Co., pp.
    184, 185-87, 256.
        Norris's unfinished trilogy demonstrates his awareness
    of America's position in world affairs at the turn of the
    century.

2   HICKS, GRANVILLE. The Great Tradition. New York: The MacMillan
    Company, pp. 168-75, passim. (Rev. ed., Chicago: Quad-
    rangle Books, 1969, pp. 168-75, passim.)
        Norris was a great pioneer in the school of realism with
    a social purpose. Unfortunately, he did not mature before
    his early death; had he lived, he might have clarified
    such confused ideas as those which mar the ending of The
    Octopus and written great reformist literature. (For re-
    sponses, see Reninger, 1940.2, and Meyer, 1943.2.)

3   LEISY, ERNEST E. AND JAY B. HUBBELL. "Doctoral Dissertations in
    American Literature," American Literature, IV (January),
    419-65.
        Lists one dissertation on Norris.

1933

4   PEIXOTTO, ERNEST. "Romanticist Under the Skin," <u>Saturday Review</u>
     <u>of Literature</u>, IX (May 15), 613–15.
         Peixotto enjoyed a long friendship with Norris in Paris,
     San Francisco, and New York; he was well acquainted with the
     backgrounds to Norris's composition of <u>Moran of the Lady</u>
     <u>Letty</u>, <u>McTeague</u>, <u>Blix</u>, <u>The Octopus</u>, and <u>The Pit</u>. In his
     opinion, Norris must be judged finally as both a realist and
     a romantic.

1934

1   BIXLER, PAUL H. "Frank Norris's Literary Reputation," <u>American</u>
     <u>Literature</u>, VI (May), 109–21.
         A survey of early critical and popular response to Norris.
     Norris's success in sales derives in part from Howell's
     early championing of him, in part from his "first rate and
     important books," <u>McTeague</u>, <u>The Octopus</u>, and <u>Vandover and</u>
     <u>the Brute</u>, and in part from his untimely death.

2   DREISER, THEODORE. "The Great American Novel" in George Jean
     Nathan, ed., <u>The American Spectator Yearbook</u>. New York:
     Frederick A. Stokes, pp. 16–25.
         Reprinted from 1932.5.

3   FRENCH, JOHN C. "Norris, Benjamin Franklin," <u>Dictionary of Amer-</u>
     <u>ican Biography</u>, VII. New York: Charles Scribner's Sons, pp.
     551–52.
         Biographical sketch of Norris, deriving chiefly from
     Walker, 1932.10, and early published memoirs.

4   GAER, JOSEPH. <u>Frank Norris (Benjamin Franklin Norris): Biblio-</u>
     <u>graphy and Biographical Data</u>. Berkeley: California Liter-
     ary Research Project No. 3.
         Includes a brief biography and an incomplete listing of
     writings by and about Norris.

5   HARTWICK, HARRY. <u>The Foreground of American Literature</u>. New
     York: American Book Company, pp. 45–66.
         Norris's "love of bulk and brawn" places him in the "main
     tradition of American Naturalism." He draws heavily on Zola
     for his effects, but he is also a product of his own period
     of robust individualism.

6   RICHARDS, GRANT. <u>Author Hunting by an Old Literary Sports Man</u>.
     New York: Coward-McCann, pp. 169–172, 174, 188.
         Richards, alledgedly quoting Norris, recounts the famous
     story of the "suppression" of <u>Sister Carrie</u>. Richards was

not won over to Dreiser at this time, but he did appreciate
Norris and had come to New York, among other reasons, "to
secure, if I could, the English rights in the future books"
of Norris.

1935

1 HATCHER, HARLAN. Creating the Modern American Novel. New York:
   Farrar and Rinehart, pp. 15-18, passim.
      McTeague, The Octopus, and The Pit clearly reveal the
   direction in which American fiction was moving at the turn
   of the century --that is, toward greater realism.

2 MARTIN, WILLARD, E. Jr. "The Establishment of the Order of
   Printings in Books Printed from Plates: Illustrated in Frank
   Norris's The Octopus," American Literature, V (March), 17-28.
      Using various impressions of The Octopus as examples,
   Martin proposes a method of "dating" plate-printings of a
   work through sight collation of individual copies. He also
   includes a descriptive bibliography of The Octopus, illus-
   trating his findings.

3 ____. "Frank Norris's Reading at Harvard College," American
   Literature, VII (May), 203-04.
      Norris's borrower's card for the Harvard College Library
   reveals a record of the books he checked out between February and June 1895. At least one of these influenced his
   current writing directly: Thomas Fillebrown's A Textbook
   of Operative Dentistry.

4 WALKER, FRANKLIN D., comp. The Letters of Western Authors, Number 3, Frank Norris. San Francisco: Johnck & Seeger.
      Walker introduces Norris's letter to Harry M. Wright,
   dated April 5, 1899, and notes that Norris's correspondence
   shows more readily than McTeague how boyish Norris was.

1936

1 GENTHE, ARNOLD. As I Remember. New York: Reynal and Hitchcock,
   p. 49, passim.
      Genthe briefly describes Norris's appearance and person-
   ality during his period with The Wave. He terms the stories
   written at this time for The Wave "brilliant."

1936

2   HARTWICK, HARRY. "Frank Norris" in Walter Fuller Taylor, A History of American Letters. New York: American Book Company, pp. 564-65.
        A short bibliography of both primary and secondary Norris material. (See 1936.5.)

3   MARTIN, WILLARD, E. JR. "Two Uncollected Essays by Frank Norris," American Literature, VIII (May), 190-98.
        Reprints two of Norris's articles written in early 1902: "'The Literature of the West:' A Reply to W. R. Lighton" and "The National Spirit as It Relates to the 'Great American Novel.'"

4   QUINN, ARTHUR HOBSON. American Fiction: An Historical and Critical Survey. New York: D. Appleton-Century Company, pp. 624-30.
        Like Crane, Davis, London, and others, Norris began his career as a journalist, but his brand of journalism differed from theirs "because he was concerned with reform, while they were either unconcerned with it or were definitely more interested in other phases of fiction." Norris turned from journalism to novels and criticism, his novels illustrating that he was fundamentally a "critic of economic and social conditions."

5   TAYLOR, WALTER FULLER. A History of American Letters. New York: American Book Company, pp. 312-315.
        A brief discussion of Norris and his works. Norris is "less consistently a pioneer naturalist" than Crane, but more believable a writer than either Crane or London. (For a response, see Reninger, 1940.2.)

1937

1   CLEATON, IRENE AND ALLEN CLEATON. Books and Battles: American Literature, 1920-1930. Boston: Houghton, Mifflin, and Co., p. 120.
        Passing reference to Norris as one of America's important writers.

2   LOGGIN, VERNON. I Hear America. New York: Thomas Y. Crowell Co., pp. 118-25, passim.
        Norris often wrote for the popular audience in the manners of Kipling, de Maupassant, and Davis; but his memorable work was modeled upon Zola's method.

1939

3   MC COLE, C. JOHN. Lucifer at Large. New York: Longmans, Green,
       and Co., pp. 24-26.
           Norris is essentially a writer of "American Naturalism."

4   MULLER, HERBERT JOSEPH. Modern Fiction. New York: Funk and
       Wagnalls Company, pp. 201-02.
           Norris was the "child of Zola." McTeague bears the "liv-
       id birthmark of naturalism." Norris, however, tired of nat-
       uralism and wrote The Octopus, which is "impressive," and
       The Pit, which is "more exciting than profound."

5   TAYLOR, WALTER FULLER. "That Gilded Age!," Sewanee Review, XLV
       (January), 41-54.   .
           Passing reference to Norris as a writer who wrote more
       freely of sex than many commentators on his period have
       suggested.

                            1939

1   KAZIN, ALFRED. "Three Pioneer Realists," Saturday Review of
       Literature, XX (July 8), 3-4, 14-15.
           As the hesitation of the nineties evolved into the hope
       of a new century, so Norris "anticipated the pattern of a
       new decade." His major literary attribute is his "delight
       in bigness," usually expressed in his incurable joie de vivre.
       He hoped to write novels which would show the greatness of
       America, but he failed to achieve his purpose in The Octopus
       and The Pit. In McTeague, however, he succeeded in reducing
       the saga of an entire "civilization into the bitter and
       remorseless drama of one dumb soul's failure."

2   SMITH, BERNARD. Forces in American Criticism. New York: Har-
       court, Brace, and Co., pp. 181-84.
           Norris's various comments on the "romantic" in fiction
       "need not be taken too seriously," for he was actually a
       part of the realistic school of American fiction. The tasks
       of the novelist which he sets forth in The Responsibilities
       of the Novelist make him the last exponent of the "militant
       realism of the democratic West."

3   "A Superb Collection of Frank Norris," Dawson's Book Shop Cata-
       logue, CXXXVIII (December), 27-28.
           Included in the catalogue is a note concerning Norris's
       habit of giving parties for friends upon the initial pub-
       lication of his books, at which he distributed advance
       copies in special bindings.

1940

1   HINKEL, EDGAR J. Criticism of California Literature, II.
     Oakland, California: Alameda County Public Library,
     pp. 669-97.
          A collection of critical excerpts about Norris as a writer
     and about some of his works.

2   RENINGER, H. WILLARD. "Norris Explains The Octopus: A Correlation
     of his Theory and Practice," American Literature, XII (May),
     218-27.
          An examination of Norris's "theory of the novel" illus-
     trates his purpose in The Octopus. Its closing sentences
     represent the only conclusion possible, given in the preced-
     ing events, and point up its complete "philosophical consis-
     tency." (A response to Hicks, 1933.2, Taylor, 1936.5, and
     Walcutt, Diss. item 37; for a rejoinder, see Walcutt, 1941.3)

3   VAN DOREN, CARL. The American Novel 1789-1939. New York: The
     Macmillan Company, pp. 233-36, passim.
          Norris's "epic inclination" allowed him to be "a leader
     in a conscious movement to continentalize American literature
     as a protest against local color." He attempted to analyze
     fundamental motives of human action.

1941

1   CARGILL, OSCAR. Intellectual America. New York: The Macmillan
     Company, pp. 89-107, passim.
          In the course of Norris's progression "up from Robert
     Louis Stevenson and Romance," he developed the "superman"
     as a permanent fixture in his novels; it is this "superman"
     who contributes to the failure of much of his work, for in
     using such a character Norris "destroyed the illusion of
     life so essential to credence in determinism."

2   NORRIS, CHARLES G. "Introduction," McTeague. San Francisco:
     Colt Press.
          This edition restores the original state of the text.
     For a discussion of the expurgated passages, see Katz and
     Manning, 1968.4.

3   WALCUTT, CHARLES C. "Frank Norris on Realism and Naturalism,"
     American Literature, XIII (March), 61-63.
          Norris's The Responsibilities of the Novelist cannot be
     read as a single unified whole; rather, it must be consid-
     ered, along with its lapses, with his other work in deter-
     mining precisely what his theory of the novel was and the
     various ways in which this theory was transferred to prac-
     tice. (A rejoinder to Reninger, 1940.2.)

1942

1   BENET, WILLIAM ROSE. "Rereading 'The Pit,'" Saturday Review of
    Literature, XXV (July 25), 17.
        Norris's prose exhibits a certain "driving power" espec-
    ially suited to painting "big canvases." He conceived bus-
    inessmen as a super-race; while we perceive his error, we are
    still fighting his battle with the traditional "big Inter-
    ests."

2   BLANCK, JACOB. Merle Johnson's American First Editions Revised
    and Enlarged. New York: R. R. Bowker Co., 399-400.
        A brief primary bibliography.

3   KAZIN, ALFRED. On Native Grounds. New York: Reynal and Hitch-
    cock, pp. 97-102, passim.
        A love of size and an overwhelming, but boyish, joy are
    Norris's two most significant attributes. Everything in his
    novels is big, a factor which explains their confusion. But
    in McTeague he succeeds, though at the expense of melodrama.

4   MARCHAND, ERNEST. Frank Norris: A Study. Stanford: Stanford
    University Press.
        The study seeks to complement the portrait of Norris as a
    writer presented by Walker in 1932.10. Norris is placed
    "against the wider background of his period--social and in-
    tellectual as well as purely literary--to examine several
    aspects of his thought and of his work." Norris's position
    regarding the movements of Romanticism, Realism, and Natural-
    ism is considered; and his preoccupations with the individ-
    ual's place in society and in the world at large at the close
    of the nineteenth century are illustrated through critical
    analyses of his novels. The study closes with an evaluation
    of Norris's exuberant style and a survey of critical reaction
    to his work.

5   MEYER, GEORGE WILBUR. "The Original Social Purpose of the Natur-
    alistic Novel," Sewanee Review, L (October-December), 563-70.
        Passing reference to Norris as a follower of Zola's true
    philosophy, the essence of which most critics have missed.

6   TAYLOR, WALTER FULLER. The Economic Novel in America. Chapel
    Hill: The University of North Carolina Press, pp. 282-306.
        Norris's novelistic career embodied, because of Zola's
    influence, a search for modern adventure which was finally
    realized in his novels about "Business." In writing these
    novels he posed two aims for himself: he must tell a good
    story; and he must enlighten "The People" with "Truth." But
    The Octopus and The Pit fail in this latter respect in that
    Norris's own "philosophical inconsistency" detracts from his

1942

second objective. (For responses, see Meyer, 1943.2, Pizer, 1955.5, and Pizer, 1963.2.)

1943

1 CURTI, MERLE. The Growth of American Thought. New York: Harper & Brothers, p. 608.
   The Octopus and The Pit are novels of social protest about "small businessmen driven to the wall by the tactics of great industrial and railway corporations."

2 MEYER, GEORGE WILBUR. "A New Interpretation of The Octopus," College English, IV (March), 341–59.
   Norris works out three central themes in The Octopus: the immutability of the natural order as represented by the wheat; the maladjustment to nature and consequent cause of evil of the late nineteenth-century American socio-economic system; and the basic need to reform that system. An examination of how these purposes are accomplished demonstrates Norris's own "philosophical consistency" in the novel as well as that of his characters. (A response to Pattee, 1915.3, Beer, 1926.1, Parrington, 1930.8, Chamberlain, 1932.3, Hicks, 1933.2, and Taylor, 1942.5.)

3 POLLOCK, CHANNING. Harvest of My Years: An Autobiography. Indianapolis: Bobbs-Merrill, pp. 73, 127–30, passim.
   Howells first brought Norris to Pollock's attention. Terming his dramatization of The Pit his "maiden effort," Pollock tells how he adapted the novel and describes the reception accorded the play.

4 STOVALL, FLOYD. American Idealism. Norman: University of Oklahoma Press, pp. 128–29.
   Because Norris was impatient with so-called "local color writing," he resorted to writing works of epic proportions. His trilogy of the "wheat," had it been completed, would have been a unique work in American literature.

1944

1 ADAMS, J. DONALD. The Shape of Books to Come. New York: Viking Press, pp. 49–52.
   Norris did not have Crane's gift for the "illuminating phrase" or the "intensely revealing situation," but he was more fully equipped for the sustained effort of novel writing. More than Crane, Norris attempted to apply Zola's method to fiction.

1947

2   STRONG, AUSTIN. "The Frank Norris," Saturday Review of Literat-
    ure, XXVII (July 1), 13.
         Strong quotes a letter from Mrs. Jeannette Black, Norris's
    widow, in which she tells of her tearful attendance at the
    launching of the Frank Norris in Richmond, California. She
    concludes that "There was a cynical side to it all, because
    none of the people knew anything about Frank Norris....But
    nothing could spoil that moment when I saw his name on that
    great ship!"

1945 (No Entries.)

1946

1   FARRELL, JAMES T. "Social Themes in American Realism," English
    Journal, XXXV (June), 309-315.
         To a large degree The Octopus reflects many of the tenets
    of agrarian populism, a social, political, and economic move-
    ment significant in post-Civil War America.

1947

1   AHNEBRINK, LARS. The Influence of Émile Zola on Frank Norris.
    Upsala: A.-B. Lundequistska Bökhandeln.
         Zola's influence on Norris is especially evident in Mc-
    Teague, Vandover and the Brute, The Octopus, and The Pit.
    Norris seems not only to have imitated Zola's style, charac-
    terizations, plots, and themes, but he also apparently bor-
    rowed directly from various parts of Zola's novels.

2   BURGUM, EDWIN BERRY. The Novel and the World's Dilemma. New
    York: Oxford University Press, pp. 158-223.
         Like Crane, Norris attempted to capture the life of the
    man of the street by a "painstaking assemblage of detail."
    Like Upton Sinclair, Norris was notable as a muckraker.

3   COWLEY, MALCOLM. "Naturalism's Terrible McTeague," New Republic
    CXVI (May 5), 31-33. In a brief, but incomplete, overview
    of Norris's life and career, Cowley characterizes Norris as
    a "giant who never grew up." However, in his short life and
    even shorter career, Norris "impress[ed] his whole personal-
    ity on Naturalism."

4   _____. "'Not Men:' A Natural History of American Naturalism,"
    Kenyon Review, IX (Winter), 414-35.
         Norris, "not Crane...set the standards for Naturalistic
    Fiction in the United States." Like "all" naturalists,

however, even Norris did not remain faithful to his credo
throughout his career.

5   CRAVEN, AVERY AND WALTER JOHNSON. The United States: Experiment
in Democracy. Boston: Ginn and Company, p. 681.
Like other naturalistic novels, McTeague, Vandover and the
Brute, and The Octopus exhibit the author's ironic tone, his
refusal to pass moral judgment on characters and situation,
and his cold, scientific temper.

6   DUFFUS, R. L. "Norris in Retrospect," New York Times Book Review,
XCVI (June 8), 5.
The reviewer finds that Norris mixes realism and romanticism almost inseparably in The Octopus. The novel represents his "protest," but it also bespeaks his faith in man's
ultimate good.

7   GEISMAR, MAXWELL. The Last of the Provincials: The American
Novel, 1915-1925. Boston: Houghton, Mifflin, and Co.,
passim.
Norris's "naturalism" was fairly influential on writers
of this period.

8   MORLEY, S. A. "Frank Norris, American Realist," Trek, XI (January
24), 16.
In spite of a "talent for vivid prose" and some passages
which contain the "seeds of greatness," Norris's art ultimately fails because it is dated: "photographic or phonographic
methods are the last that the true artist thinks of using."

9   SNELL, GEORGE. The Shapers of American Fiction, 1798-1947. New
York: E. P. Dutton & Co., Inc., pp. 226-33, passim.
Norris was the foremost early champion of American naturalism, but while his novels do disclose many techniques borrowed
from Zola, they also contain a liberal amount of romance.
Norris's inconsistencies of personality are thus reflected
as thematic inconsistencies in his work.

10 WALCUTT, CHARLES C. "Frank Norris and the Search for Form,"
University of Kansas City Review, XIV (Winter), 126-36.
All of Norris's major serious novels fail because he is
unable to discover a viable method of uniting human free
will and naturalistic theory. (For a response, see Pizer,
1955.5.)

11 WITHAM, W. TASKER. Panorama of American Literature. [New York]:
Stephen Daye Press, pp. 217-219, passim.
Norris was the naturalistic successor to Crane; as a novel-
ist he was interested in describing men's "animal instincts."

1948

1   COWIE, ALEXANDER. The Rise of the American Novel. New York:
    American Book Company, pp. 699, 746, 749.
        As a follower of Howells, Norris added strength to the
    Realistic movement; as a proletarian and naturalist writer,
    his technique was too "florid."

2   LEARY, LEWIS, comp. "Doctoral Dissertations in American Literat-
    ure," American Literature, XXII (May), 169-230.
        Lists two dissertations on Norris.

3   MC KEE, IRVING. "Notable Memorials to Mussel Slough," Pacific
    Historical Review, XVII (February), 19-27.
        Though justifiably the most famous, The Octopus was actu-
    ally the second of three "memorials" to Mussel Slough.
    Norris seems to have followed the basic facts religiously,
    but he opposed general public feeling of the time toward the
    massacre by not wholly condemming the Southern Pacific Rail-
    road.

4   SPILLER, ROBERT E., and others. Literary History of the United
    States, II. New York: The MacMillan Company, pp. 1026-33,
    passim.
        Though he scorned the so-called "realistic" school in his
    published criticism and allied himself to that of "Romance,"
    Norris was closer to Howells than he thought. Zola influenced
    Norris's work to a marked degree, but "his love of the story
    for itself" prevented his ever writing purely "scientific
    naturalism." His best work was written during his college
    years when he was composing McTeague and Vandover and the
    Brute. (For a response, see Pizer, 1955.5).

5   _____., eds. "(Benjamin) Frank(lin) Norris, "Literary History
    of the United States: Bibliography, III. New York: The
    MacMillan Company, pp. 668-69.
        Lists the more important studies of Norris up to 1948,
    but lists no reviews of individual works.

6   TEBBEL, JOHN. George Horace Lorimer and The Saturday Evening
    Post. Garden City: Doubleday, pp. 35, 45.
        At a luncheon engagement F. Scott Fitzgerald bemoans to
    Isaac Marcosson, Lorimer, and others, the lack of critical
    and editorial insight in American magazines. Lorimer re-
    plies: "Then maybe I didn't go so far wrong after all when
    I bought 'The Pit' and 'The Octopus' from Frank Norris and
    serialized them both in the Post."

1948

7   WALCUTT, CHARLES C. "The Naturalism of Vandover, and the Brute,"
    in William Van O'Connor, ed., Forms of Modern Fiction.
    Minneapolis: University of Minnesota Press, pp. 254-68.
        Vandover and the Brute possesses the possibility of
    "modern tragedy," which exists between the poles of "mechan-
    istic determinism" and benignant nature. The novel is weak,
    but its very weakness illustrates the potential strength of
    naturalism.

                              1949

1   BECKER, GEORGE J. "Realism: An Essay in Definition," Modern
    Language Quarterly, X (June), 184-97.
        McTeague is an example of the "realistic method" carried
    to an extreme.

                              1950

1   AHNEBRINK, LARS. The Beginning of Naturalism in American Fic-
    tion: A Study of the Works of Hamlin Garland, Stephen Crane,
    and Frank Norris with Special Reference to Some European In-
    fluences, 1891-1903. Upsala: A.-B. Lundequistska Bokhandeln;
    Cambridge: Harvard University Press.
        An expansion in part of his earlier study (see 1947.1).
    Like Crane and Garland, Norris owed a debt not only to Zola,
    but also to Ibsen and Turgenev. In addition, Norris seems
    to have borrowed from Huysmans. But, despite his kinship to
    Crane and Garland with respect to continental influences,
    Norris was a different sort of novelist from them. Garland
    and Crane can both safely be termed "realistic" whereas
    Norris was a "Zolaesque naturalist."

2   COLLINS, CARVEL. "Introduction," McTeague: A Story of San Fran-
    cisco. New York: Holt, Rinehart and Winston, Inc., pp. vii-
    xviii.
        Though heavily influenced by Zola, Norris did not make
    McTeague a "slavish" imitation of his master. Using the es-
    tablished tenets of French naturalism, including materialism,
    determinism, and pessimism, Norris described in the Novel the
    "destruction of an 'innocent.'" The novel is essentially
    "moralistic," but Norris succeeds, nevertheless, in compos-
    ing a modern American "tragedy."

3   COMMAGER, HENRY STEELE. The American Mind: An Interpretation
    of American Thought and Character Since the 1880's. New
    Haven: Yale University Press, pp. 60, 109, 111-13.
        Norris's brand of determinism, like London's, was violent
    and "confused."

1951

4   COWLEY, MALCOLM. "Naturalism in American Literature" in Stow
        Persons, ed., Evolutionary Thought in America . New Haven:
        Yale University Press, pp. 300-33.
            Largely reprinted from 1947.3 and 1947.4.

5   JONES, ARTHUR E. JR. "Darwinism and its Relationship to Realism
        and Naturalism in American Fiction, 1860 to 1900" Drew Uni-
        versity Bulletin, XXXVIII (December), 1-21.
            In many demonstrable respects Norris reflects the influ-
        ence of Darwin in his novels. Though Norris never synthe-
        sized his own position as to naturalism, realism, and roman-
        ticism, he nonetheless employs obviously Darwinian techniques
        throughout his work.

6   KAZIN, ALFRED. "American Naturalism: Reflections from Another
        Era" in Margaret Denny and William H. Gilman, eds., The
        American Writer and the European Tradition. Minneapolis:
        University of Minnesota Press, pp. 121-31.
            Despite the power of McTeague, the reader may find it
        "curiously repellent" less because of its subject than be-
        cause of Norris's "patronizing" attitude toward his material.

7   WILSON, EDMUND. Classics and Commercials. New York: Farrar,
        Strauss,and Company, p. 50.
            Passing reference that Steinbeck borrowed a scene from
        McTeague for his Of Mice and Men.

                            1951

1   DEEGAN, DOROTHY YOST. The Stereotype of the Single Woman in
        American Novels. New York: Columbia University Press, pp.
        96, 141-42.
            Vandover and the Brute is one of the few nineteenth cen-
        tury American novels in which a woman--in this case, Flossie-
        engages in "some unconventional sex relationship." Miss
        Baker in McTeague is "one of the best-drawn single-woman
        characters" in American fiction.

2   GLICKSBURG, CLARKES I. American Literary Criticism, 1900-1950.
        New York: Hendricks House, Inc., p. 7.
            The Responsibilities of the Novelist "was eagerly accepted
        by the young naturalists of the time as a manifesto voicing
        their aesthetic creed."

1951

3   HOFFMAN, FREDERICK J. The Modern Novel in America, 1900-1950.
        Chicago: Henry Regnery Company, pp. 32-40, passim.
            Norris's work exhibits many of the general characteristics
        of traditional naturalism: need for documentation; "tension"
        in physical action; mastery of fact; obsession for "the great
        American novel;" and portrayal of the superman.

4   KNIGHT, GRANT C. The Critical Period in American Literature.
        Chapel Hill: University of North Carolina Press, pp. 161-68,
        passim.
            "McTeague, within its scope, is such a novel as Zola might
        have composed about San Francisco." It helped win a victory
        for American realists who determined to rebel against Howells
        and other followers of the genteel tradition.

5   MATTHIESSEN, F. O. Theodore Dreiser. New York: Sloane, pp.
        58-59, passim.
            Rather than predictably chronicling Norris's role in the
        publication of Sister Carrie, Matthiessen delivers various
        statements about Norris as a naturalist.

6   QUINN, ARTHUR HOBSON, ed. The Literature of the American People.
        New York: Appleton-Century-Crofts, pp. 749-54, passim.
            In general Norris possessed a "boyish want of sagacity."
        While McTeague and The Octopus are notable for their "unusual
        scope, vitality, and imagery," they and his other works are
        marred by his own mental contradictions.

1952

1   BROOKS, VAN WYCK. The Confident Years: 1885-1915. New York:
        E. P. Dutton & Company, pp. 217-36, passim.
            The influence of Zola is very apparent in Norris's work.
        Norris is particularly interested in characterization, al-
        though in McTeague his characters are often "types." Unfor-
        tunately, too, his "naturalism" forced him to go out of his
        way to show the absence of free will in men.

2   ["GRADY, JIM"]. "Frank Norris," "This Is San Francisco" [a CBS
        radio series on KCBS, San Francisco.] [October (?).]
            Part of advertising campaign for a current exhibit of
        Norris material at Berkeley; suggests that Norris drew his
        characters from actuality.

1953

3   HORTON, ROD W. AND HERBERT W. EDWARDS. Backgrounds of American
     Literary Thought. New York: Appleton-Century-Crofts, p.
     259.
          Norris mentioned as an "outstanding" naturalist.

4   O'CONNOR, WILLIAM VAN. An Age of Criticism: 1900-1950. Chi-
     cago: Henry Regnery Company, pp. 41-42.
          Despite Norris's support of Zolaesque naturalism, he real-
     ized that "Zola's laws...were not absolutes;" he used natur-
     alistic techniques as convenient means by which he might
     achieve his primary objective of writing "good stories."

5   SCHERMAN, DAVID E. AND ROSEMARIE REDLICH. Literary America: A
     Chronicle of American Writers from 1607-1952 with 173 Photo-
     graphs of the American Scene that Inspired Them. New York:
     Dodd, Mead, & Co., p. 88.
          As a naturalist Norris was interested neither in "deter-
     minism" nor true "objectivity;" rather, he was concerned with
     the "individual."

6   WAGENKNECHT, EDWARD C. Cavalcade of the American Novel. New
     York: Holt, Rinehart and Winston, Inc., pp. 216-22, passim.
          While he wrote one bad book and experienced artistic lap-
     ses in all his novels, Norris's "achievement" is yet consid-
     erable and impressive.

7   WEST, RAY B. JR. The Short Story in America: 1900-1950. Chi-
     cago: Henry Regnery Company, pp. 18, 30-34.
          Norris was typical of the early naturalists but distin-
     guished by "bold portrayals of life and by rigid social and
     political attitudes." His shorter writings have been for-
     gotten--and "rightly so."

1953

1   GEISMAR, MAXWELL D. Rebels and Ancestors. Boston: Houghton,
     Mifflin and Company, pp. 3-66.
          Norris's novels eloquently represent his efforts to
     shuck off the "typical standards and superstitions of his
     youthful background, as well as...the destructive elements
     in his own temperament."

2   KAPLAN, CHARLES. "Norris's Use of Sources in The Pit," American
     Literature, XXV (March), 75-84.
          Even though Norris recreates Joseph Leiter's "spectacular"
     career in the "pit" through close attention to detail, he
     alters both incident and characterization in order to am-

plify the basic drama of his novel. Thus, wherever possible, Norris capitalizes upon Jadwin's magnitude, always depicting him as a single man against the all-encompassing wheat.

3 KWIAT, JOSEPH J. "The Newspaper Experience: Crane, Norris, and Dreiser," Nineteenth Century Fiction, VIII (September), 99-117.

Like his contemporaries, Crane and Dreiser, Norris's "newspaper experience" on the Wave was invaluable in his later career as a "serious" writer, for in their early phases of reportorial work all three writers acquired a facility for the observation and the reporting of events and for recognizing the difficulties of human existence. (For a response, see Katz, 1971.5.)

4 "The Search Continues for Missing Pages of Lost Manuscript," California Monthly (March), pp. 19, 37-38.

Briefly relates the beginnings of James D. Hart's search for the McTeague manuscript and gives a short biographical sketch of Norris.

1954

1 CARTER, EVERETT. Howells and the Age of Realism. Philadelphia: J. B. Lippincott Company, pp. 246-49, passim.

Howells realized that Norris's work, especially McTeague and The Octopus, ran far afield from the type of fiction he had endeavored to establish in America; nevertheless, he encouraged Norris, praising him with "words which had not been heard in American criticism since Emerson." McTeague was a "personal epic," while The Octopus Howells called an Iliad to McTeague's Odyssey.

2 COWLEY, MALCOLM. The Literary Situation. New York: Viking Press, pp. 75-77, passim.

Norris "would be the first American novelist to become a formal convert to naturalism and, with a few infidelities, to cherish its doctrines to the end." Norris adopted many of Zola's techniques and carried them to extremes in his own work.

3 CUNLIFFE, MARCUS. The Literature of the United States. Baltimore: Penguin Books, pp. 218-19, passim.

In Norris's writings, realism and romanticism are mingled with the "Darwinian literary attitude." His most ambitious work is The Octopus which exhibits real narrative power; yet it also shows his confused mode of thought.

1955

4 KAPLAN, CHARLES. "Fact into Fiction in McTeague," Harvard Library
    Bulletin, VIII (Autumn), 381–85.
        Many passages of a technical nature in McTeague can be
    traced directly to Thomas Fillebrown's A Text-book of Oper-
    ative Dentistry, which Norris checked out while studying at
    Harvard. In some cases Norris quotes this textbook almost
    verbatim.

5 KNIGHT, GRANT C. The Strenuous Age in America. Chapel Hill:
    University of North Carolina Press, pp. 41–48, passim.
        The Octopus is a "sum of contradictions," but it is still
    a "great novel."

6 KWIAT, JOSEPH J. "Frank Norris: The Novelist as Social Critic
    and Literary Theorist," Die Neueren Sprachen, IX, 385–92.
        Although Norris possessed many distinct social ideals, he
    was usually unable to reconcile them with his equally distinct
    aesthetic theories. Yet his novelistic career represents an
    important and enlightening picture of a struggle not uncommon
    for many writers.

7 LEARY, LEWIS, comp. Articles on American Literature, 1900–1950.
    Durham, North Carolina: Duke University Press, pp. 222–23.
        Lists forty-two articles on Norris.

1955

1 CLARK, HARRY HAYDEN. "The Influence of Science on American Lit-
    erary Criticism, 1860–1910," Wisconsin Academy of Sciences,
    Arts, and Letters, XLIV, 109–64.
        In his work, Norris exhibits a debt to the "evolutionists,"
    but he is not consistent, and he is equally influenced by
    writers who expounded opposing theories.

2 HOFFMAN, CHARLES G. "Norris and the Responsibility of the Novel-
    ist," South Atlantic Quarterly, LIV (October), 508–15.
        Norris perceived the responsibility of the novelist as a
    moral concept: an underlying but cohesive theme in all his
    novels is "moral regeneration through the power of love."
    The novel must have a message, and this message should appeal
    in the long run to the taste which the public should have.

3 HOFSTADTER, RICHARD. The Age of Reform: From Bryan to FDR.
    New York: Alfred A. Knopf, p. 200.
        Passing reference to The Octopus as a novel of "reality."

1955

4   LYNN, KENNETH S. The Dream of Success: A Study of the Modern
    American Imagination. Boston: Little, Brown and Co., pp.
    158-207.
        A bookish, shy, and indecisive son of an agressive and
    dynamic father, Norris repeatedly attempted to expiate the
    guilt he felt for disappointing him. Because of this mo-
    tive, Norris worshipfully created heroic father-figures and
    celebrated "manly" success in his writings. Dominated by
    his literary mother, Norris fashioned his heroines as asex-
    ual creatures; and, because he remained a little boy in re-
    lation to his mother, he gave his heroines the large phys-
    ical attributes that a child would visualize when thinking
    of his mother.

5   PIZER, DONALD. "Another Look at 'The Octopus,'" Nineteenth-
    Century Fiction, X (December), 217-24.
        Through the struggles of Presley and the epiphanies of
    Vanamee and Annixter, Norris accomplishes a dual purpose
    in The Octopus: the perception of "Truth" can be individ-
    ual, and a benevolent nature aids in discovering this
    "Truth." (A response to Parrington, 1930.8, Taylor 1942.5,
    Walcutt, 1947.10, and Spiller, 1948.4.)

6   SPILLER, ROBERT E. Cycle of American Literature. New York:
    The Macmillan Company, pp. 201-04, passim.
        Norris was torn by a nexus of conflicting ideals, beliefs,
    and influences, which makes even his best work vague.

1956

1   BROOKS, VAN WYCK AND OTTO L. BETTMAN. Our Literary Heritage:
    A Pictorial History of the Writers in America. New York:
    E. P. Dutton & Company, Inc., p. 213, passim.
        The influence of San Francisco on Norris's boyhood is
    highly apparent in his novels, in which he celebrated force.
    As founder of the "'red-blood' school" in American liter-
    ature, Norris rebelled against established practices in
    fiction of the nineties.

2   CRANE, MAURICE A. "The Case of the Drunken Goldfish," College
    English, XVII (February), 309-10.
        Norris's determination to be "real" causes him to miss
    the humor of Hawthorne's "The Great Carbuncle" and thus to
    make Trina "an absurd figure."

1957

3   PIPER, HENRY DAN. "Frank Norris and Scott Fitzgerald," Hunting-
    ton Library Quarterly, XIX (August), 393-400.
        Fitzgerald's early work demonstrates a lasting debt to
    Norris's Vandover and the Brute. The vacillating Fitzgerald
    worshipped Norris in 1919-20, as a kind of artistic master.
    Norris's influence waned with time, but Fitzgerald's letters
    and papers reveal that throughout his life he held Norris
    and his work in high regard.

4   WALCUTT, CHARLES C. American Literary Naturalism: A Dividend
    Stream. Minneapolis: University of Minnesota Press, pp.
    114-56, passim.
        Incorporates 1947.10 and 1948.7 with the addition of gen-
    eral biographical matter and a short discussion of The Pit.
    The thesis is identical in all three studies: Norris's nov-
    els fail structurally, even with their many excellences,
    because he never devised a way to mesh effectively his ideas
    concerning free will on the one hand and "traditional" nat-
    uralism on the other.

5   WALKER, FRANKLIN D., ed. The Letters of Frank Norris. San Fran-
    cisco: The Book Club of California.
        Walker discusses to some degree nearly every one of the
    letters or other Norris items he includes in this volume,
    observing that "nearly always the subject of the letters is
    [Norris's] writing."

                            1957

1   CHASE, RICHARD V. The American Novel and Its Tradition. Garden
    City: Doubleday, pp. 185-204.
        Norris is a thoroughly "naturalistic" writer, whose
    novels depict "the degeneration of characters under the
    pressure of heredity and environment," and whose penchant
    for "mythic ideology" closely relates him to the late nine-
    teenth-century vogue of Populism.

2   COOLIDGE, JOHN S. "Lewis E. Gates: The Permutations of Roman-
    ticism in America," New England Quarterly, XXX (March),
    23-38.
        Gates's realization of the later nineteenth century as a
    period of literary quest to bring down the "Vision on the
    Mount...into the rumouring, turbulent life below" allowed
    him to discern, perhaps better than Norris himself, the
    implications of McTeague, and to recognize the novel as the
    end product of the literary revolution he himself was de-
    scribing. Gates's theories of literature also explain
    Norris's method of documentation and choice of subject in
    McTeague.

1957

3   KNIGHT, ARTHUR. The Liveliest Art: A Panoramic History of the
    Movies: New York: The Macmillan Company, pp. 139-41.
        Interprets McTeague from Erich von Stroheim's point of
    view as a subject for a great film exposing human frailty.

4   LUNDY, ROBERT D. "Introduction," The Octopus. New York: Hill
    and Wang, Inc.
        Places The Octopus in the context of Norris's career
    through 1901, describes its composition, and discusses its
    factual background.

5   MC CORMICK, JOHN. Catastrophe and Imagination: An Interpretation
    of the Recent English and American Novel. New York: Longman,
    Green, and Co., pp. 111-12, passim.
        Norris attempted to make naturalism romantic.

6   POCHMANN, HENRY A. German Culture in America: Philosophical and
    Literary Influences, 1600-1900. Madison: University of
    Wisconsin Press, p. 482.
        Passing reference to Norris as a proponent of Hamlin Gar-
    land's "veritism."

7   SMITH, GUY E. American Literature: A Complete Survey. Totowa,
    New Jersey: Littlefield, Adams, & Co., pp. 137-38, 220-21.
        Presents brief plot summaries of McTeague, Vandover and
    the Brute, The Octopus, and The Pit, as well as general
    comments on Norris as a member of the vanguard of naturalism.

1958

1   CADY, EDWIN H. The Realist at War. Syracuse: Syracuse Uni-
    versity Press, pp. 218-22, passim.
        While not a "follower" of Howells or even a "Realist,"
    Norris shared with Howells a dislike for "faked, pilfered
    romanticisms" and a strong desire for truthful fiction.
    Not surprisingly, then, Howells came to admire Norris's
    work.

2   GOLDSMITH, ARNOLD L. "The Development of Frank Norris's Phil-
    osophy" in A. Doyle Wallace and Woodburn O. Ross, eds.,
    Studies in Honor of John Wilcox. Detroit: Wayne State Uni-
    versity Press, pp. 175-94.
        Norris's "philosophy" neatly falls into four distinct
    periods beginning with his "pessimistic naturalism" of 1891-
    95 and concluding with the restricted optimism of The Octopus
    and The Pit.

3   HART, JAMES D. "Search and Research: The Librarian and the
    Scholar," College and Research Libraries, XIX (September),
    365-74.

Hart reveals many of the ways through which the Frank
Norris Collection, housed in The Bancroft Library, University of California, Berkeley, was built.

4   LYNN, KENNETH S.   "Introduction," The Octopus. Boston: Houghton,
    Mifflin Company, pp. v-xxv.
        By "any architectonic standard, The Octopus is a literary
    chaos." Coherence, however, is achieved by the "terrific
    energy" with which Norris develops the stories of Annixter,
    Presley, and Vanamee: the result is an "epic," and Norris's
    best novel. This energy grew out of Norris's desire to re-
    solve his own problem as an American intellectual and writer
    of the 1890s. Upon his three heroes, he projects his need
    to break out of personal isolation from life and into a ful-
    filling relationship with a "pulsing vital universe," the
    "real" world of action.

5   PIZER, DONALD. "Romantic Individualism in Garland, Norris and
    Crane," American Quarterly, X (Winter), 463-75.
        Largely a repeat of 1955.5 with the conclusion that Nor-
    ris's belief in "intuitively derived Truth" qualifies him as
    an exponent of the American tradition of "romantic individ-
    ualism."

6   SHERWOOD, JOHN R. "Norris and the Jeannette," Philological
    Quarterly, XXXVII (April), 245-52.
        In the setting, subject matter, and dialogue of A Man's
    Woman, Norris borrowed extensively from books written about
    the disasters suffered by the crew of the Jeannette during
    a polar expedition in 1879-91; he also drew from at least
    one other account of Arctic exploration. Yet Norris is to
    be commended for constructing a very skilful adaptation
    of his source material.

7   SPILLER, ROBERT E., et al., eds. "(Benjamin) Frank(lin) Norris,"
    Literary History of the United States: Bibliography Supple-
    ment. New York: The Macmillan Company, p. 172.
        A supplement to 1948.5.

                              1959

1   BLANKENSHIP, RUSSELL. American Literature as an Expression of
    the National Mind., rev. ed. New York: Henry Holt, pp. 513,
    516, 527-32.
        Norris moves from a naturalism highly indebted to Zola
    but intermixed with numerous romantic elements in McTeague
    and Vandover and the Brute to an unfortunate concern for
    "sociology" in The Octopus and The Pit, which is an "example
    of what a naturalist can produce when he becomes too much
    interested in sociology."

1959

2   COOPERMAN, STANLEY. "Frank Norris and the Werewolf of Guilt,"
     Modern Language Quarterly, XX (September), 252-58.
         McTeague and Vandover and the Brute reflect less Norris's
     application of the new ideas of scientific determinism to
     traditional Calvinistic determinism than the exact opposite:
     Norris so feared sins of the flesh that his ideal "pure"
     love is "asexual."

3   ELIAS, ROBERT H., ed. Letters of Theodore Dreiser: A Selection.
     Philadelphia: University of Pennsylvania Press, passim.
         Norris appears in Dreiser's correspondence infrequently
     and usually in references to his part in promoting the pub-
     lication of Sister Carrie.

4   FALK, ROBERT P. "From Poor Richard to the Man in the Gray Flan-
     nel Suit: A Literary Portrait of the Businessman," California
     Management Review, I (Summer), 1-14.
         Norris expresses his belief in the "cult of the strong"
     man with the character of Jadwin, who embodies all the ex-
     citement and gambling of stock-market speculation. Norris's
     hero possesses some characteristics of Poor Richard and
     Horatio Alger's protagonists, but Jadwin has no use for the
     Christian ethic.

5   FRANCIS, H. E. "A Reconsideration of Frank Norris," Emory Uni-
     versity Quarterly, XV (June), 110-18.
         Norris's best work is marred by his inability "to recon-
     cile the novelist with the moralist." Yet his works are
     still significant for their youthful exuberance which
     truly reflects his romantic nature.

6   HART, JAMES D. "Search and Research: The Librarian and the
     Scholar," Book Club of California Quarterly News-Letter,
     XXIV (Spring), 27-34.
         Reprinted from 1958.3.

7   LOHF, KENNETH A. AND EUGENE P. SHEEHY. Frank Norris: A Biblio-
     graphy. Los Gatos, California: Talisman Press.
         First attempt at a comprehensive description and enumer-
     ation of both primary and secondary Norris material.

8   MARCOSSON, ISAAC F. Before I Forget: A Pilgrimage to the Past.
     New York: Dodd, Mead, & Co., pp. 500-509, passim.
         Largely reprinted from 1920.1.

9   MARX, LEO.   "Two Kingdoms of Force," <u>Massachusetts Review</u>, I
    (October), 62–95.
        Norris, like many other major American writers, dramatizes
    in <u>The Octopus</u> a basic contradiction in the American ideal:
    an overriding faith in industrial progress is expressed, yet
    industrialism is constantly depicted in violent struggles
    against nature, which is also revered. (For a response,
    see Pizer, 1963.2.)

10 MILLGATE, MICHAEL.   "The Novelist and the Businessman: Henry
    James, Edith Wharton, Frank Norris', <u>Studi Americani</u>, V,
    161–89.
        Norris's <u>The Pit</u> fulfills nearly all the criteria which
    Henry James cited as being necessary for an American business
    novel. Although Norris seems to have accomplished his task
    with great help in theme and plot from Zola's <u>L'Argent</u>, his
    novel is still underrated.

11 TODD, EDGELEY, W.   "The Frontier Epic: Frank Norris and John G.
    Neihardt," <u>Western Humanities Review</u>, XIII (Winter), 40–45.
        Neihardt's <u>A Cycle of the West</u>, itself based upon his
    own carefully worked out theory of epic literature, perhaps
    was written "as a genuine attempt to compensate for the ne-
    glect of the Western epic Frank Norris complained of, at the
    same time that it fulfills the aspirations he once dreamed
    of in <u>The Octopus</u>."

12 WHITE, WILLIAM.   "Frank Norris: Bibliographical Addenda," <u>Bul-
    letin of Bibliography</u>, XXII, 227–28.
        A supplement to 1959.7.

                              1960

1   DILLINGHAM, WILLIAM B.   "Frank Norris and the Genteel Tradition,"
    <u>Tennessee Studies in Literature</u>, V, 15–24.
        Although Norris indeed opposes the "genteel tradition" in
    several respects, such as his choice of subject matter, his
    attention to "unpleasant details," and his belief in Darwin-
    ism, he nevertheless exemplifies some characteristics of that
    tradition, particularly in regard to his treatment of his
    heroines, in all his novels.

2   GEISMAR, MAXWELL.   <u>Writers in Crisis</u>: <u>The American Novel, 1925–</u>
    <u>1940</u>. Boston: Houghton, Mifflin, and Co., p. 265.
        Passing reference to Norris as a literary ancestor of
    John Steinbeck.

1960

3   LEARY, LEWIS, ed. <u>American Literary Essays</u>   New York: Thomas Y.
     Crowell Company, pp. 247-250.
         Norris believed fiction had a purpose and called his work
     romantic because it did not take ordinary people for its
     subject.

4   NYREN, DOROTHY, ed. <u>A Library of Literary Criticism</u>: <u>Modern
     American Literature</u>. New York: Frederick Ungar Publishing
     Co., pp. 358-61.
         Brief excerpts from a few critics of Norris and his work.

5   THORP, WILLARD. <u>American Writing in the Twentieth Century</u>. Cam-
     bridge: Harvard University Press, pp. 158-61, <u>passim</u>.
         Throughout his brief career as a novelist, Norris "never
     sorted out his convictions. In the same work romantic ep-
     isodes jostle Spencerian doctrine and socialistic theories."
     Norris acquired the naturalistic creed through his reading,
     his thinking, and his "revolt, with some guilt in the pro-
     cess, against the gentility to which he had been born."

6   WALKER, FRANKLIN D. "An Early Frank Norris Item," Book Club of
     California <u>Quarterly News-Letter</u>, XXV (Fall), 83-86.
         Walker presents the earliest known letter by Norris, a
     petition requesting a change in his student status at Berke-
     ley; by his sophomore year, Norris "had abandoned any in-
     tention of getting a degree, preferring to concentrate on a
     background for writing." (See Walker, 1970.12 for another
     introduction to this same letter.)

1961

1   DILLINGHAM, WILLIAM B. "The Old Folks of <u>McTeague</u>," <u>Nineteenth
     Century Fiction</u>, XVI (September), 169-73.
         Many critics have failed to discover an integral signi-
     ficance of the secondary plot in <u>McTeague</u> involving Old Gran-
     nis and Miss Baker and have dismissed this sub-plot as a
     lapse on Norris's part; but the Grannis-Baker episodes in
     reality constitute an important illumination of the theme
     of chance in the novel.

2   GERSTENBERGER, DONNA AND GEORGE HENDRICK. <u>The American Novel,
     1789-1959</u>. <u>A Checklist of Twentieth Century Criticism</u>.
     Denver: Alan Swallow, pp. 207-09.
         Lists fifty-three articles on Norris.

3   JOHNSON, GEORGE W. "Frank Norris and Romance," <u>American Liter-
     ature</u>, XXXIII (March),· 52-63.
         Although Norris contributed much to the infant literary
     techniques of naturalism, he endeavors in his best work to
     unite romance, e.g., "large abstractions," vast themes, es-

1962

cape imagery, etc., with realism, e.g., "careful observation,"
dramatic method, structural parallels, etc.

4   KAZIN, ALFRED. Contemporaries. Boston: Little, Brown, and Co.,
     pp. 92-93.
          While Dreiser presented a vitalistic vision of life with
     his "loving realism," Norris, a "pseudo-Nietzchean natural-
     ist," insisted on depicting a world hostile to man.

5   PIZER, DONALD. "Evolutionary Ethical Dualism in Frank Norris'
     Vandover and the Brute and McTeague," PMLA, LXXVI (December),
     552-60.
          Both McTeague and Vandover and the Brute fit an evolution-
     ary scheme in that Vandover regresses to an earlier stage by
     yielding to the "brute" within himself, while McTeague's
     atavistic tendencies toward "degeneracy" never permit him
     to evolve adequately enough to combat his own inner "brute."
     Yet Norris is justified in holding Vandover culpable for
     his downfall on the one hand, and in absolving McTeague of
     responsibility for his descent on the other.

1962

1   ANDO, SHOICHI. "Characteristics of Frank Norris' Works," Review
     of English Literature, XI (March), 113-39.
          Describes Norris's most salient features as a novelist:
     his realism, his naturalistic viewpoint, and exuberant melo-
     dramatic romanticism.

2   FOLSOM, JAMES K. "Social Darwinism of Social Protest? The 'Phil-
     osophy' of The Octopus," Modern Fiction Studies, VIII (Win-
     ter), 393-400.
          The "illogical" ending of The Octopus may be explained as
     an ironic technique: neither Presley nor Vanamee understands
     the real heart of the fight between railroad and ranchers,
     which is that the profit motive ought to govern the actions
     of both groups.

3   FRENCH, WARREN G. Frank Norris: New York: Twayne Publishers,
     Inc.
          In this critical biography of Norris all of his major
     works are treated. Norris was essentially a Romantic, "a
     scion of the transcendentalists," and his works can be in-
     terpreted in that light. In his very moralistic writings,
     he used the techniques of "the imported naturalistic tra-
     dition" for the purpose of "refurbishing the nearly moribund
     tractarian tradition." The study closes with a resume of
     critical reaction to Norris.

1962

4   HILL, JOHN S. "Poe's 'Fall of the House of Usher' and Frank
         Norris' Early Short Stories," Huntington Library Quarterly,
         XXVI (October), 111-12.
             Poe, whose influence is "apparent" in two early short
         stories by Norris--"His Single Blessedness" and "A Case
         for Lombroso"--"should now be added to the list of writers
         who may have influenced" Norris.

5   _____. "Trina Sieppe: First Lady of American Literary Natural-
         ism," University of Kansas City Review, XXIX (October),
         77-80.
             Not only is Trina McTeague the "first" fully-developed
         female character in American literature to fall victim to
         the naturalistic effects of heredity and environment, but
         she also must answer for causing the ultimate downfall of
         her husband.

6   JOHNSON, GEORGE W. "The Frontier Behind Frank Norris' McTeague,"
         Huntington Library Quarterly, XXVI (November), 91-104.
             The proverbial "loss of the frontier" in America was of
         primary significance to Norris who in McTeague struggles
         with the paradox of a mythical "bumpkin." In all of his
         novels, in fact, Norris constructs situations in which his
         main characters must conquer essential antipodes.

7   KIRK, CLARA M. AND RUDOLF KIRK. William Dean Howells New York:
         Twayne Publisher, Inc., passim.
             Passing references to Howells's practice of reviewing
         the works of Norris and other promising young writers.

8   KWIAT, JOSEPH J. "Frank Norris: the Novelist as Social Critic
         and Literary Theorist," Arizona Quarterly, XVIII (Winter),
         319-28.
             Reprinted from 1954.6.

9   PIZER, DONALD. "The Concept of Nature in Frank Norris' The
         Octopus," American Quarterly, XIV (Spring), 73-80.
             The theme and structure of The Octopus illustrates
         Norris's familiarity with the beliefs held by evolutionary
         theists. The wheat functions as the representation of
         divine force in the novel, allowing men either to perceive
         truth or to reject its lessons.

10   _____. "Frank Norris' Definition of Naturalism," Modern Fiction
         Studies, VIII (Winter), 408-10.
             Naturalism bridges the gap between realism and romanti-
         cism. From realism it takes accuracy of detail; from roman-
         ticism it borrows depth of philosophy. But it is dissimilar
         to both in its distinctive choice of subject matter, accord-
         ing to Norris.

1964

11 _____ . "Ten Letters by Frank Norris," Book Club of California
Quarterly News-Letter, XXVII (Summer), 51-61.
The letters presented constitute a "sizable addition to
the canon of Norris' correspondence," both for biographical
and bibliographical reasons.

12 SCHNEIDER, ROBERT W. "Frank Norris: the Naturalist as Victorian,"
Midcontinent American Studies Journal, III (Spring), 13-27.
Contrary to the opinions of many critics, Norris was not
a thoroughgoing rebel; rather, his ideas, as his writings
indicate, were deeply entrenched in the genteel tradition
of his day. He honored a Victorian sexual code and believed
in freedom of will.

13 WALCUTT, CHARLES C. "Norris, [Benjamin] Frank[lin]" in Max J.
Herzberg, et al., eds., The Reader's Encyclopedia of American
Literature . New York: Thomas Y. Crowell Co., pp. 807-08.
Brief biographical evaluation of Norris. Considers
Norris more interested in Zola as novelist than as natural-
ist, and pleads that he should not be "underrated" as a ser-
ious writer.

1963

1 LYON, PETER. Success Story. The Life and Times of S. S. Mc-
Clure. New York: Charles Scribner's Sons, pp. 153-53, 173-
74, passim.
Norris was hired by the S. S. McClure Company in 1899
but was unsuccessful as a correspondent in Cuba. On January
9, 1900, Norris wrote to John Phillips, telling him his reasons for leaving McClure to work for Doubleday.

2 PIZER, DONALD. "Synthetic Criticism and Frank Norris; Or, Mr.
Marx, Mr. Taylor, and The Octopus," American Literature,
XXXIV (January), 532-41.
Norris neither pits industrialism against nature, nor
does he emphasize the misuse of the railroad and other mech-
anistic symbols of progress in The Octopus; rather, he op-
poses trusts such as that represented by the railroad. His
theme is that technology and nature, "'resistlessly work
together for good.'" (A response to Taylor, 1942.5 and Marx,
1959.9.)

1964

1 BLAIR, WALTER, et al. American Literature: A Brief History.
New York: Scott, Foresman and Company, passim.
In The Octopus and The Pit, Norris acts as a social crit-
ic, given to expressing himself through symbols.

91

1964

2   CARGILL, OSCAR. "Afterword," The Octopus. New York: New
    American Library, pp. 459-69.
        Norris intended to write an expose of railroad trusts,
    and his initial research was done in this direction. How-
    ever, the split between Doubleday and McClure and a conver-
    sation with the mighty Huntington swayed him to construct
    a novel which placed equal blame on the opposing factions.

3   CHILDS, JAMES. "The First Draft of McTeague: 1893," American
    Notes and Queries, III (November), 37-38.
        Basing his conclusion on internal evidence, Childs sug-
    gests that McTeague was begun during the winter vacation of
    Norris's junior year, 1893, at Berkeley.

4   DAVISON, RICHARD ALLEN. "Frank Norris's Thirteen Uncollected
    News-letters," Notes and Queries, N. S., XI (February), 71-73.
        The thirteen uncollected newsletters constitute "ample
    new material...for a reexamination of Norris's aesthetics."

5   HILL, JOHN S. "The Writing and Publication of the Novels of
    Frank Norris," American Notes and Queries, II (June), 151-52.
        A concise listing of the publication, serialization,
    and probable composition dates of Norris's seven novels.

6   MARX, LEO. The Machine in the Garden: Technology and the Pas-
    toral Ideal in America. New York: Oxford University Press,
    pp. 16, 343-44.
        The section on Norris is a revision of 1959.9.

7   MAY, HENRY F. The End of American Innocence. Chicago: Quad-
    rangle Books, pp. 48, 189, 201.
        Passing references to Norris as a Zolesque naturalist.

8   MILLGATE, MICHAEL. American Social Fiction: James to Cozzens.
    New York: Barnes and Noble, pp. 38-53, passim.
        Norris owes much to Howells and Zola, especially in The
    Pit. That he was ultimately concerned with the "responsi-
    bility of the novelist" qualifies him more as a significant
    exemplar of social awareness than as a follower of the ro-
    mantic tradition.

9   PIZER, DONALD, ed. The Literary Criticism of Frank Norris.
    Austin: University of Texas Press.
        Pizer rejects Franklin Walker's opinion that Norris had
    no "coherent intellectual position" as a critic and suggests
    that the basic coherence "underlying Norris' criticism is a
    primitivistic anti-intellectualism." Pizer groups Norris's
    critical essays in ten sections in order to explain this
    coherence.

1965

10   _____ . "The Masculine-Feminine Ethic in Frank Norris' Popular
      Novels," Texas Studies in Literature and Language, VI, 84-91.
         Norris's three "middle" novels form a rudimentary trilogy
      in which he explores the correct roles of man and woman: man
      must be strong in mind and body; woman must aid man in over-
      coming his weaknesses, must surrender to his superior
      strength, and must balance femininity with her own portion
      of masculinity.

11   REXROTH, KENNETH. "Afterword," McTeague: A Story of San Franc-
      isco. New York: New American Library, pp. 341-48.
         Now that we have some historical distance from McTeague,
      we can more easily recognize that "the writing is easy and
      natural, the moral earnestness refreshing, and the construc-
      tion masterful." Norris's characters are "bright and clear"
      and his symbolism is "intensely dramatic." McTeague is
      especially enjoyable because of its externality to the Pro-
      testant-Romantic-Existentialist novelistic tradition; Norris
      stands outside this school of intensely self-conscious
      writers.

                              1965

1   BERTHOFF, WARNER. The Ferment of Realism: American Literature,
      1884-1914. New York: The Free Press, pp. 223-27, passim.
         Norris's "continuing reputation as a serious figure in
      American literature is hard to understand." His crimes
      against literary taste include inabilities to write "credible
      dialogue," to conceive interesting plots, to describe appeal-
      ing characters, and to write original fiction. His "rep-
      utation as a novelist seems an accident of publicity."

2   CARGILL, OSCAR. Toward a Pluralistic Criticism. Carbondale,
      Illinois: Southern Illinois University Press, pp. 118-30.
         Reprinted from 1964.2.

3   COLLINS CARVEL. "Frank Norris, McTeague: A Story of San Franc-
      isco" in Wallace Stegner, ed., The American Novel from James
      Fenimore Cooper to William Faulkner. New York: Basic Books,
      Inc., pp. 97-105.
         A revision of 1950.2.

4   MALIN, IRVING, ed. Psychoanalysis and American Fiction. New
      York: E. P. Dutton and Company, pp. 187-198.
         Reprints excerpts from Geismar, 1953.1.

1965

5   MORGAN, H. WAYNE. "Frank Norris: The Romantic as Naturalist"
       in American Writers in Rebellion from Mark Twain to Dreiser.
       New York: Hill and Wang, Inc., pp. 104-45.
          Norris was basically "a romantic dealing with naturalis-
       tic techniques rather than naturalistic ethics." He never
       mastered his craft fully, but he was a vigorous, if some-
       times confused, writer who "infused fresh vitality, sheer
       energy, into American letters."

6   PIZER, DONALD. "Nineteenth-Century American Naturalism: An
       Essay in Definition," Bucknell Review, XIII (December), 1-
       18.
          Where Dreiser, and Crane even moreso, seek to demonstrate
       that the sensational aspects of life occur so frequently
       that they become dull and trivial, Norris in McTeague strives
       to show that the extraordinary underlies anyone's placid
       existence and may erupt violently at any moment.

7   SCHNEIDER, ROBERT W. Five Novelists of the Progressive Era.
       New York: Columbia University Press, pp. 112-52, passim.
          An expansion of 1962.12. A great deal more of Norris's
       work, especially his early efforts, is treated here.

8   STRAUMANN, HEINRICH. American Literature in the Twentieth
       Century. 3rd ed. New York: Harper and Row, pp. 31-32.
          Norris is typical of many American determinists: he can-
       not refrain from expressing some optimism, as is the case
       in The Octopus.

9   SWANBERG, W. A. Dreiser. New York: Charles Scribner's Sons,
       pp. 87-90, passim.
          Norris fought for Dreiser's rights in the publication of
       Sister Carrie.

1966

1   DAVISON, RICHARD ALLEN. "An Unpublished Norris Discussion of
       Kipling," American Notes and Queries, IV (February), 87.
          Davison suggests that Norris may have been an able critic
       of poetry and reprints "Frank Norris' Weekly Letter," Chi-
       cago American: Art and Literary Review (June 29, 1901), p. 8.

2   HOLMAN, C. HUGH, comp. The American Novel through Henry James
       New York: Appleton-Century-Crofts, pp. 66-68.
          A brief enumerative bibliography of Norris.

1966

3   PIZER, DONALD. The Novels of Frank Norris. Bloomington:
         Indiana University Press.
             Norris believed in an evolutionary philosophical system
         and constructed his novels around that system and out of
         that belief. Yet his writings also contained ideas which
         served to weaken his system. For instance, his "masculine-
         feminine ethic" seriously detracts from the major themes of
         his novels. Even so, his "positive view of man and society,"
         his optimistic delight in the forces of good, and his
         imaginative intensity continue to recommend him as an im-
         portant novelist in American Literature—one whose ideas
         seem not too foreign to our own.

4   _____. Realism and Naturalism in Nineteenth-Century American
         Literature. Carbondale: Southern Illinois University Press.
             Includes the following: "Late Nineteenth-Century American
         Naturalism," pp. 11-32, reprinted from 1956.6; "Frank Norris's
         Definition of Naturalism," pp. 33-36, reprinted from 1962.10;
         "The Significance of Frank Norris's Literary Criticism," pp.
         99-107, largely reprinted from "Introduction Section I" in
         1964.9; and "Synthetic Criticism and Frank Norris's The
         Octopus," reprinted from 1963.2.

5   STONE, EDWARD. Voices of Despair. Athens: Ohio University
         Press, pp. 57-62, 119-20, passim.
             Like Zola, Norris often portrays human beings as mere
         animals in an unsympathetic world.

6   WALKER, FRANKLIN D. "Frank Norris and Jack London," Mills Col-
         lege Magazine (Spring), pp. 15-23.
             Although London and Norris were close in age, attended
         the University of California at Berkeley at times not far
         removed from each other, and began writing at about the
         same time, the two are not really similar in many important
         respects. In temperament, style, and mood, their works
         differ sharply. Furthermore, their early material shows
         little indication that either had read the work of the other.

7   ZIFF, LARZER. The American 1890s: Life and Times of a Lost Gen-
         eration. New York: Viking Press, pp. 250-74, passim.
             In his best work, Norris employs Zolaesque methods to
         good effect in that he penetrates "within the habitation to
         the soul's secrets." As Norris hurried through his short
         life, he strove to distinguish between the life he wished
         to penetrate and the literature he superficially disdained,
         but the distinction was always more apparent than real. When
         he did realize a difference, he dangerously approached not
         virile life, but bad art.

1967

1   FRENCH, WARREN. "Frank Norris (1870-1902)," <u>American Literary
     Realism</u>, I (Fall), 84-89.
         Cursorily evaluates some major criticism of Norris, notes
     the Norris holdings in various libraries, and isolates areas
     of Norris's work which merit further attention.

2   GOLDSMITH, ARNOLD L. "Charles and Frank Norris," <u>Western Ameri-
     can Literature</u>, II (Spring), 30-49.
         Charles Norris's eleven novels reveal a striking debt to
     Norris, a better and more famous writer. Charles's reverence
     for his brother was nearly overwhelming, and he gratified it
     by drawing upon the latter's adventuresome life and major
     writings for style, plot, characterizations, themes, even
     for "philosophical ideas."

3   HART, JAMES D. "The Frank Norris Home, San Francisco" in Albert
     Shumate and Oscar Lewis, eds., <u>Homes of California Authors</u>.
     San Francisco: Book Club of California, No. 6.
         Norris's home played a role in both <u>Vandover and the
     Brute</u> and <u>McTeague</u>.

4   MARTIN, JAY. <u>Harvests of Change: American Literature, 1865-
     1914</u>. Englewood Cliffs, New Jersey: Prentice-Hall, pp. 70-
     77, <u>passim</u>.
         Norris was neither a scientific naturalist nor a muck-
     raker; rather, the main trait of his writing was its re-
     peated celebration of "the romance of force." In <u>The
     Octopus</u>, Norris came close to writing the "National Novel."

5   WALKER, DON D. "The Western Naturalism of Frank Norris," <u>West-
     ern American Literature</u>, II (Spring), 14-29.
         Norris's favorite theme is the "presence of the brute
     beneath the veneer of civilization." In nearly all of his
     novels he works out this theme by pitting his protagonists
     against huge canvasses--deserts of sand or ice, wheat fields,
     coastlines, the sea--and causing them to reflect upon their
     primeval pasts.

6   WALKER, FRANKLIN D. "Three More Frank Norris Petitions," Book
     Club of California <u>Quarterly News-Letter</u>, XXXIII (Winter),
     10-12.
         Walker amends his earlier conclusion that Norris's pe-
     tition for a change in his student status was granted (see
     1960.6), and presents three new petitions from Norris to
     the University of California authorities concerning various
     problems Norris encountered in his program of study at
     Berkeley.

7 WALKER, PHILIP. "The Octopus and Zola: a New Look," Symposium, XXI (Summer), 155-65.
  Norris does indeed adapt much of Zola's work to the needs of The Octopus. Yet where the mature Zola developed a grand vision based on his transformation of observation and detail into omnipresent, pervasive symbolism, Norris's imagery never rose above the rhetorical, the romantic, the more obviously grandiose. The difference between Norris and Zola, therefore, may be more significant than their superficial similarities.

1968

1 ASTRO, RICHARD. "Vandover and the Brute and The Beautiful and Damned: A Search for Thematic and Stylistic Reinterpretations," Modern Fiction Studies, XVI (Winter), 397-413.
  The charge of Fitzgerald's failure in The Beautiful and Damned can be exonerated when its extensive parallels in theme, characterization, style, and ultimate purpose to Norris's Vandover and the Brute are isolated and explored. Evidently, Fitzgerald drew heavily on Norris in all these areas.

2 DAVISON, RICHARD ALLEN, ed. "The Remaining Seven of 'Frank Norris' Weekly Letters,'" American Literary Realism, III (Summer), 47-65.
  Davison presents seven of Norris's "letters" written for the Chicago American: Art and Literary Review and comments that the letters should be of invaluable aid to Norris scholars not only as primary Norris material but also for Norris's "assessment of the contemporary literary scene" in them.

3 _____. "An Undiscovered Early Review of Norris' Octopus," Western American Literature, III, 147-51.
  Davison reprints Wallace Rice's review of The Octopus (see 1901.28), commenting that Rice makes the typical complaints about the repetitive quality of the novel, its "misshapen structure," and its wrong-headed morality. He is the first of many critics to identify Norris with Presley and to fail to see the irony of Shelgrim's speech; but, like other reviewers, he acknowledges Norris's power.

4 KATZ, JOSEPH AND JOHN J. MANNING. "Notes on Frank Norris's Revision of Two Novels," Papers of the Bibliographical Society of America, LXII (Second Quarter), 256-59.

Respect for Norris's "professionalism" must increase when one considers his considerable talent for revision, as demonstrated in McTeague and A Man's Woman.

5   LABRIE, RODRIQUE E. "The Howells-Norris Relationship and the Growth of Naturalism," Discourse: A Review of the Liberal Arts, XI (Summer), 363-70.
    Despite the broad influence of Zola and other European naturalists on late nineteenth-century American writers, Norris was the only one who both admitted his debt to Zola and consciously strove to inculcate so-called "Zolaistic" principles in his work. Howells, above all, recognized the parallels between Norris and Zola, yet he still had the foresight to encourage, even to champion, Norris, who himself respected Howells but viewed his novels as being essentially "teacup tragedies."

6   MACKAY, MARGARET. The Violent Friend: The Story of Mrs. Robert Louis Stevenson. Garden City: Doubleday & Company, Inc., p. 503.
    Fanny Stevenson erected a "memorial seat" to Norris, a good friend, along the pathway to his cabin. She and Norris also recorded their voices on a phonograph record before his death.

7   NOBLE, DAVID W. The Eternal Adam and the New World Garden. New York: George Braziller, pp. 105-15.
    Norris's "novels form a pattern which reveals his sustained effort to move from the shock of acceptance of man's continued imperfection to the optimistic outlook that finally this inner weakness was to be transcended through the benevolent, if harsh, influence of evolutionary nature." Chance dictates events in Vandover and the Brute and McTeague, novels in which the protagonists fall prey to their inherently evil natures; but in The Octopus Norris affirms his faith in progress and in the final redemptive goodness of nature-- a goodness which amplifies the corresponding inherent goodness in mankind.

8   WAGER, WILLIS. American Literature: A World View. New York: New York University Press, pp. 170-72, passim.
    Norris's literary efforts helped "to demonstrate" the work of Zola in America.

1969

9   WOODRESS, JAMES. Dissertations in American Literature, 1891-
     1966. Durham, North Carolina: Duke University Press, un-
     paged.
          Lists   twenty-one dissertations on Norris.

10   WOODWARD, ROBERT H.   "Frank Norris and Frederic: a Source for
     McTeague", Frederic Herald, II (April), 2.
          The most convincing evidence that Norris used Seth's
     Brother's Wife as a source for McTeague is the similarity be-
     tween parallel passages in the novels in which Seth and Mc-
     Teague watch the mass movement of a purposeful humanity on
     the street.

                              1969

1   CURLEY, DOROTHY NYREN, MAURICE KRAMER, AND ELAINE FIALKA KRAMER,
     comps., A Library of Literary Criticism: Modern American
     Literature, II. 4th ed. New York: Frederick Ungar Publish-
     ing Co., pp. 423-28, 490-91.
          A revision of 1960.4; also includes a skeletal biblio-
     graphy of primary material.

2   DAVISON, RICHARD ALLAN, comp. The Merrill Studies in The Octo-
     pus. Columbus, Ohio: Charles E. Merrill Publishing Company.
          A collection of "statements" on The Octopus in three sec-
     tions: "Letters by Frank Norris" (three); "Reviews of The
     Octopus" (nine); and "Criticism and Scholarship" (fourteen
     essays and excerpts from books.) The statements mainly il-
     lustrate the continuing controversy over the philosophical
     consistency and structural quality of the novel. "Perhaps
     the only constant in all the commentary is the enthusiastic
     acknowledgement of the power and scope" of The Octopus.

3   DILLINGHAM, WILLIAM B. Frank Norris: Instinct and Art. Lin-
     coln: University of Nebraska Press.
          In this study of Norris's life and works the general the-
     sis that Norris was a Naturalist in his vision of the world
     and in his literary techniques is presented. There are
     three sections. "Life and Career" deals with the facts of
     Norris's life, especially his training as a painter and his
     activities as a writer. "Themes" treats Norris's preoccu-
     pation with masculinity, instinct, and the "darker" aspects
     of experience in man's life through critical analyses of
     Norris's works. "Form and Style" focuses on the character-
     istics of Norris's works--style, point of view, symbolism--
     and his theory and practice in regard to the "mechanics of
     fiction." The study concludes with an annotated "Selected
     Bibliography."

1969

4   FLORY, CLAUDE REHARD. Economic Criticism in American Fiction 1792-
    1900. New York: Russell & Russell, pp. 225-26.
        Norris believed in creating "a broad canvas" and tracing
    upon it those "forces that are elemental in the life of a
    whole people." His interest lay in man in general, yet he
    managed to create many "distinctly individual" characters.

5   FROHOCK, W. M. Frank Norris. Minneapolis: University of Minne-
    sota Press.
        In this biographical and critical essay, Norris is de-
    picted as being profoundly influenced by Zola, though Norris
    never approached Zola's achievement. Norris was a more-or-
    less talented writer who made melodramatic use of naturalistic
    methods of composition.

6   GILES, JAMES R. "Beneficial Atavism in Frank Norris and Jack
    London," Western American Literature, IV (Spring), 15-27.
        In Moran of the Lady Letty, Norris cogently expresses his
    belief in "beneficial atavism," that is, that the "Anglo-Saxon
    brute" lurks underneath the surface of the "civilized man,"
    and that, given the right conditions, this "brute" may over-
    shadow his counterpart. However, only when such a reversal
    occurs in a frontier setting will it be constructive. This
    complex nexus of ideas apparently influenced much of London's
    early fiction.

7   KATZ, JOSEPH. "Frank Norris's Replies to Autograph Collectors,"
    Book Club of California Quarterly News-Letter, XXXXIX (Summer),
    58-60.
        Perhaps Norris devised a "form" response which he sent to
    persons seeking his autograph.

8   TAYLOR, GORDON O. The Passages of Thought: Psychological Repre-
    sentation in the American Novel, 1870-1900. New York: Oxford
    University Press, pp. 136-45, passim.
        Norris's method in McTeague is essentially "psychological"
    in that he "purports to be 'watching the symptoms' of interior
    change in McTeague." McTeague, though a very forceful person-
    ality, is actually driven by a primal force much greater than
    his own mere human strength.

1970

1   BERRY, THOMAS ELIOT. The Newspaper in the American Novel, 1900-
    1969. Metuchen, New Jersey: The Scarecrow Press, Inc., pp.
    39-40.
        Places Norris as a lesser star among such muckrakers as

Phillips, Herrick, and Sinclair; sees Norris as being aware
of the "power of the press" in his writings.

2   GERSTENBERGER, DONNA AND GEORGE HENDRICK. The American Novel.
    Chicago: The Swallow Press, Inc., pp. 279-82.
        A revision of 1961.2; lists sixty-eight articles on Norris.

3   HART, JAMES D., ed. A Novelist in the Making: A Collection of
    Student Themes, and the Novels Blix and Vandover and the
    Brute. Cambridge: Harvard University Press.
        From Norris's year at Harvard forty-four of his student
    themes written for English 22 survive. Since almost all
    of these themes relate in some way to Vandover and the Brute,
    McTeague, or Blix, and since these three novels contain sim-
    ilarities of plot, scene, and character, Norris quite pos-
    sibly originally conceived all three of them as aspects of a
    single work, which he attempted to write under the tutelage
    of Professor Lewis E. Gates at Harvard.

4   _____. "Introduction," The Pit. Columbus, Ohio: Charles E.
    Merrill Publishing Company, pp. v-xv.
        In The Pit Norris seeks to employ the dual techniques of
    "meticulous realism" and "spacious symbolism" which he first
    used in The Octopus. Thus, he makes the novel "epic" by
    using grandiose imagery and pretentious language.

5   HILL, JOHN S., comp. Checklist of Frank Norris. Columbus, Ohio:
    Charles E. Merrill Publishing Company.
        A selected checklist on Norris comprising six sections:
    "Books and Major Separate Publications," "Editions," "Let-
    ters," "Bibliographies and Checklists," "Biographies," and
    "Scholarship and Criticism."

6   _____. "The Influence of Cesare Lombroso on Frank Norris's Early
    Fiction," American Literature, XLII (March), 89-91.
        Norris employs aspects of the theories of Lombroso for
    "dramatic effect" in some of his early short stories, all
    published before any of his novels.

7   HOGAN, WILLIAM. "A Frank Norris Centennial at UC," San Francisco
    Chronicle, (April 9) [page number not available.]
        In connection with an exhibit mounted at The Bancroft
    Library, Berkeley, of Norris memorabilia, a private screening
    of Von Stroheim's "Greed" was held.

1970

8   KATZ, JOSEPH. A Frank Norris Collection. Columbia: University
     of South Carolina, Department of English Bibliographical
     Series, No. 5.
          A catalogue of a Norris exhibition from Katz's private
     collection mounted March 5-12 at the McKissick Library, Uni-
     versity of South Carolina, to commemorate the centenary of
     Norris's birth. Supplements Lohf and Sheehy, 1959.7.

9   LEARY, LEWIS, comp. Articles on American Literature, 1950-1967.
     Durham, North Carolina: Duke University Press, pp. 411-12.
     Lists forty-two articles on Norris.

10   LUTWACK, LEONARD. Heroic Fiction: The Epic Tradition and Amer-
     ican Novels of the Twentieth Century. Carbondale: Southern
     Illinois University Press, pp. 23-46.
          In The Octopus Norris presents four "heroes," each the
     center of a literary form. Using epic allusions and tech-
     niques, he conceives a work of "prodigal" proportions in
     which characters play against a background of economic and
     biologic gods.

11   NILON, CHARLES H. Bibliography of Bibliographies in American
     Literature. New York: R. R. Bowker Co., p. 227.
          Lists only a few bibliographies of Norris, omitting Gaer,
     1934.4, Pizer, 1966.3, and French, 1967.1.

12   PIZER, DONALD. "The Problem of Philosophy in the Novel," Buck-
     nell Review, XVIII (Spring), 53-62.
          Norris's use of "philosophy" in Vandover and the Brute
     functions primarily as a vehicle by which the "artist can
     transform a quasi-philosophical idea into evocative metaphor."
     While Norris often indulges in "overstated philosophical
     ideas," he usually does so in order to amplify the themes
     of his work.

13   STRONKS, JAMES B. "John Kendrick Bangs Criticizes Norris's Bor-
     rowings in Blix," American Literature, XLII (November), 380-
     86.
          That Norris borrowed from A. Conan Doyle as well as from
     other sources for Blix is undeniable, but Bangs may have
     overdone his contempt, considering the "featherweight love
     story" which Blix is. (See Bangs, 1899.4.)

1971

14 VANCE, WILLIAM L. "Romance in The Octopus," Genre, III (June), 111-36.

> The Octopus fails because Norris unsuccessfully introduced incompatible literary "modes" into a single work. Like Norris, Presley envisioned the greatness of each of these modes and sought to transmit his vision to writing. But both Presley and Norris failed in their tasks. The Octopus is simply too "literary" a work to be structurally sound.

15 WALKER, FRANKLIN D. Frank Norris Petitions the President and Faculty of the University of California. Berkeley: The Council of the Friends of the Bancroft Library.

> While the Academic Council of the University of California, Berkeley, never approved Norris's request for a change in his student status, it did permit him to remain four years at the University and to receive an "honorable dismissal." Norris's experience at Berkeley significantly shaped his ideas about his talent and his aspirations. (See Walker, 1960.6, for another introduction to this same petition.)

16 WHEELER, OTIS B. "The Sacramental View of Love in the Nineteenth and Twentieth Centuries" in Thomas A. Kirby and William J. Olive, eds., Essays in Honor of Esmond Linworth Marilla. Baton Rouge: Louisiana State University Press, pp. 346-49.

> If one expects purely "positivistic" naturalistic values in The Octopus, he will be disappointed. In Vandover and the Brute and McTeague Norris does depict human sexuality in positivistic or animalistic terms, but in The Octopus "sexuality is approached as a mystery," taking on "religious overtones."

1971

1 BAIRD, NEWTON D. AND ROBERT GREEN. An Annotated Bibliography of California Fiction, 1664-1970. Georgetown, California: Talisman Literary Research, pp. 340-43.

> Brief annotations of Norris's "California" novels, and several of his articles and short stories.

2 BURNS, STUART L. "The Rapist in Frank Norris's The Octopus," American Literature, XLII (January), 567-69.

> That Father Sarria is "the Other" who rapes the first Angèle is not only apparent from many verbal clues in The Octopus, but it is also provided for thematically in that Vanamee's restoration to good through evil parallels the harvest of life-giving wheat from the assaulted earth.

1971

3   CADY, EDWIN H. The Light of Common Day. Bloomington: Indiana
    University Press, pp. 44-45, 66-68, passim.
        Though Norris was not a naturalist, "the sensibility of
    the naturalist exerted a magnetic pull" on him, as it did
    on other realists of his period. Norris also felt an urge
    to revive the ancient genre of the epic, but his bathetic
    The Octopus is an embarrassing product of this urge.

4   DICKINSON, A. T. Jr. American Historical Fiction. 3rd ed. Me-
        tuchen, New Jersey: The Scarecrow Press, Inc., pp. 166-67.
        Annotates McTeague, The Octopus, and The Pit.

5   DILLINGHAM, WILLIAM B. "Frank Norris" in Robert A. Rees and
        Earl N. Harbert, eds., Fifteen American Authors Before 1900:
        Bibliographic Essays on Research and Criticism. Madison:
        University of Wisconsin Press, pp. 307-32.
        Analyzes Norris scholarship at five levels: "Bibliography,"
    "Editions," "Manuscripts and Letters," "Biography," and
    "Criticism," and concludes that the "several decades of
    criticism on Norris have by no means exhausted the possibil-
    ities for study." Norris embodied the contradictions of his
    period, was even completely a product of his time, yet was
    able "to see life from a larger prespective with a clear,
    honest vision."

6   EICHELBERGER, CLAYTON L., comp. A Guide to Critical Reviews of
        United States Fiction, 1870-1910. Metuchen, New Jersey:
        The Scarecrow Press, pp. 232-33.
        Lists forty-two reviews of Norris's novels.

7   KATZ, JOSEPH. "Frank Norris and 'The Newspaper Experience,'"
        American Literary Realism, IV (Winter), 73-77.
        Unlike Crane and Dreiser, who early in life were forced
    to support themselves as space-rate reporters on large com-
    mercial dailies, Norris "worked under a shelter" throughout
    his life. Norris himself recognizes in a letter, dated
    December 2, 1901, the fundamental difference between his
    own experience and that of more orthodox reporters. (A
    response to Kwiat, 1953.3.)

8   STRONKS, JAMES B. "Frank Norris's McTeague: A Possible Source
        in H. C. Bunner," Nineteenth Century Fiction, XXV (March),
        474-78.
        Internal evidence suggests that Norris borrowed the gen-
    eral outlines as well as some specific details of the Old
    Grannis-Miss Baker sub-plot in McTeague from H. C. Brunner's
    popular story, "The Love Letters of Smith."

9   SWENSSON, JOHN K.   "'The Great Corner in Hannibal and St. Jo:'
    A Previously Unpublished Short Story by Frank Norris,"
    American Literary Realism, IV (Summer), 205-226.
        In presenting "The Great Corner in Hannibal and St. Jo,"
    Swensson notes that as with his other attempts of economic
    fiction Norris researched this story thoroughly. The sur-
    viving manuscript probably represents a working draft.

10 WYATT, BRYANT N.   "Naturalism as Expediency in the Novels of
    Frank Norris," The Markham Review, II (February), 83-87.
        Norris relied on the techniques of "naturalism" in order
    to explain the various themes of his novels. As his career
    progressed, he resorted to the "crutch" which naturalism
    represented for him less frequently.

1972

1   BUDD, LOUIS J.   "The Hungry Bear of American Realism," American
    Literary Realism, V (Fall), 485-87.
        Commenting on Cady's definition of realism in 1971.3,
    Budd suggests that more stress should be placed upon "real-
    ism's growing attention to the pleasures, needs, and very
    presence of the body." Among other examples of this ten-
    dency in realistic fiction, he cites Norris's vivid present-
    ation of the various meals in McTeague.

2   DEW, MARJORIE.   "Realistic Innocence: Cady's Footnote to A Def-
    inition of American Literary Realism," American Literary
    Realism, V (Fall), 487-89.
        In responding to Cady's definition of realism in 1971.3,
    Dew agrees with the notion that the realists expressed an
    "'active disbelief in the health and safety of romantic in-
    dividualism,' or but positively, a belief in solidarity, so-
    cial complicity, and shared social vision." She cites Pres-
    ley's transcending of the naturalistic world-vision to "the
    hope and trust in love on earth" in The Octopus as an example
    of this belief. Like Dreiser and Crane, Norris thus compro-
    mised his "naturalism"; the three writers were governed by
    "'anti-naturalistic loyalties to man.'"

3   GOLDMAN, SUZY BERNSTEIN.   "McTeague: The Imagistic Network,"
    Western American Literature," VII (Summer), 83-99.
        Critics have noted how gold, animal, and machine imagery
    give unity to McTeague. But there are many image patterns--
    such as "food, liquid, fights, teeth, hands, prisons or
    bonds, and music"--that have gone unnoticed. Consideration
    of these patterns "proves that Norris was a far more con-

scious artist than we have yet realized." It also shows that
the much criticized conclusion of McTeague is integral to
the novel's imagistic structure.

4   KANE, NORMAN. "Corrections in the Publisher's Copy of The Pit,"
    Papers of the Bibliographical Society of America, LXVI
    Fourth Quarter), 435.
        A copy of The Pit [owned by Joseph Katz] with the book-
    plate of Walter H. Page contains pencilled comments and cor-
    rections which were made in later printings. Kane lists
    four corrections.

5   KATZ, JOSEPH. "The Manuscript of Frank Norris' McTeague: A
    Preliminary Census of Pages," Resources for American Liter-
    ary Study, II (Spring), 91-97.
        The McTeague manuscript was dispersed in 1928 when a full
    or partial sheet was inserted in each of 245 sets of the
    Argonaut Manuscript Limited Edition of Frank Norris' Work.
    The manuscript is in the process of being recovered. Katz
    supplies a list of recovered pages, their owners, and their
    relation to the first edition text of McTeague.

6   MC CLUSKEY, JOHN E. "Frank Norris' Literary Terminology: A Note
    on Historical Context," Western American Literature, VII
    (Summer), 148-50.
        Modern critics tend to think of Zola and Howells as "con-
    freres in the international battle for realism," and thus
    they have concluded that Norris was illogical in seeing the
    two as representatives of opposing schools. But Norris was
    not illogical; writers and critics of Norris's time did see
    the two men as antithetical to one another in their literary
    beliefs.

7   SMITH, DOROTHY J. "The American Railroad Novel," The Markham
    Review, III (October), 68-70.
        Unlike his predecessors in the subgenre of railroad fic-
    tion, Norris sought to do more than merely entertain. In
    The Octopus he showed that someone could "create something
    distinguished from an expose." What especially distinguishes
    The Octopus from works like Twain's tongue-in-cheek The Gild-
    ed Age is the presence of well-formed social conscience; the
    "earnestness" and "humorless intensity" of the work make it
    remarkable.

8   WATSON, CHARLES S. "A Source for the Ending of McTeague," Amer-
     ican Literary Realism, V (Spring), 1973-74.
          Internal evidence supports the possibility that the ending
     of McTeague derives from Dante's Inferno.

9   WEINBERG, HERMAN G., comp. "Foreword," The Complete Greed of
     Erich von Stroheim: A Reconstruction of the Film in 348
     Still Photos Following the Original Screenplay, Plus 52
     Production Stills. New York: Arno Press, unpaged.
          "McTeague is a story of the disintegration of character in
     the lives of ordinary people...on the lower middle-class eco-
     nomic level, who had a compulsion for money and a lust for
     gold which they could not control....It is a work of unparal-
     leled ferocity in its relentless hammering upon the theme
     of money as money and gold as gold." Yet its characters are
     not just "freaks," for Norris does draw them with pity as
     suffering human beings.

1973

1   DAVIDSON, MARSHALL B., ed. The American Heritage History of the
     Writers' America. New York: American Heritage Publishing
     Company, Inc., pp. 239-41, passim.
          Because Norris was acquainted with the work of Howells,
     Davis, and Crane, he emulated them on the one hand in his
     fiction, and, on the other, rebelled against them as liter-
     ary models. While not a stylist, he did develop a "rude
     strength" in his popular works.

2   GRAHAM, D. B. "Studio Art in The Octopus," American Literature
     XLIV (January), 657-66.
          In ridiculing the salon artists of his day in The Octopus
     Norris focussed specifically on Yone Noguchi, one of the
     popular poets associated with Gelett Burgess on The Lark.

3   ISANI, MUKHTAR ALI. "Jack London on Norris' The Octopus," Amer-
     ican Literary Realism, VI (Winter), 66-69.
          Reprints London's review of The Octopus (see 1901.13) and
     opines, "The review is especially noteworthy for its clear
     pointers toward the esthetic and socialistic bases of Lon-
     don's obvious admiration for Norris who had preceded him into
     naturalism." Relates that London also found Moran of the
     Lady Letty "well done."

4   KATZ, JOSEPH. "The Elusive Criticisms Syndicated by Frank Nor-
      ris," Proof 3, 221-52.
         Eight syndicated critical pieces by Norris listed in the
      bibliography included in The Responsibilities of the Novel-
      ist have puzzled Norris scholars for seventy years because
      appearances of them have not been discovered. Seven of the
      eight have now turned up, as well as one essay, previously
      unknown. The text of these essays is presented here.

5   ____ . "The Shorter Publications of Frank Norris: A Checklist,"
      Proof 3, 155-220.
         Katz presents a considerably expanded enumeration of
      Norris's short pieces with the conclusion that the Norris
      reflected in this checklist is rather different from the
      one with whom most scholars and students are familiar. Nor-
      ris was prolific both as writer and illustrator in the form
      of drawings, photographs, and paintings. A complete record
      of his work will probably never be achieved, but not all
      possible sources for it have been exhausted or examined yet.

6   SPANGLER, GEORGE M. "Eliot's 'Red Rock' and Norris's 'McTeague,'"
      Notes and Queries, N. S. XX (September), 330-31.
         Norris's reference in the penultimate chapter of McTeague
      to "a pile of red rock" may be the source of a similar refer-
      ence in the first section of The Waste Land. Both works are
      pervaded with a sense of "dryness, sterility, sleeplessness,
      and fear;" both writers express an interest in the "primitive
      man, the bestial triumphant over the moral and spiritual."

DOCTORAL DISSERTATIONS

1   BELLER, HILLIARD I. "Values and Antinomies in the Novels of Frank Norris." New York University, 1970.

2   BERANEK, HENRIETTE. "Das 'Gilded Age' im Romanwerk des Frank Norris." University of Vienna, 1951.

3   BERNSTEIN, SUZY J. "The Novels of Frank Norris: An Analysis of Their Structure." Columbia University, 1970.

4   BUCHESKY, CHARLES S. "The Background of American Literary Naturalism." Wayne State University, 1971.

5   CRISLER, JESSE S. "A Critical and Textual Study of Frank Norris's McTeague." University of South Carolina, 1973.

6   DAVISON, RICHARD A. "Frank Norris' Aesthetic Theory and Artistic Practice." University of Wisconsin, 1964.

7   DICKERSON, LYNN C. "The Dispossessed Character: Elements of Irony and Compassion in American Literary Naturalism at the Turn of the Century." Emory University, 1969.

8   DILLINGHAM, WILLIAM B. "Themes and Literary Techniques in the Fiction of Frank Norris." University of Pennsylvania, 1961.

9   EDMONDSON, ELSIE F. L. "The Writer as Hero in Important American Fiction since Howells." University of Michigan, 1954.

10   FIGG, ROBERT M. "The Effect of Naturalism Upon Form in the American Novel from 1893 to 1925." University of North Carolina, 1965.

11   FINK, SISTER MARY J. "The Concept of the Artist and Creative Genius in American Naturalistic Fiction." University of Notre Dame, 1965.

Doctoral Dissertations

12 GARDNER, JOSEPH H. "Dickens in America: Mark Twain, Howells, James, and Norris." University of California, Berkeley, 1969.

13 GARDNER, SARA J. H. "Social Thought in the Writings of Frank Norris." Washington State University, 1966.

14 GARSON, HELEN S. "The Fallen Woman in American Naturalistic Fiction: From Crane to Faulkner." University of Maryland, 1967.

15 GILES, JAMES R. "A Study of the Concept of Atavism in the Writings of Rudyard Kipling, Frank Norris, and Jack London." University of Texas, 1967.

16 GINANNI, FRANCIS R. "Impressionistic Techniques in the Novels of Frank Norris." Auburn University, 1970.

17 GOLDSMITH, ARNOLD L. "Free Will, Determinism, and Social Responsibility in the Writings of Oliver Wendell Holmes, Sr., Frank Norris, and Henry James." University of Wisconsin, 1953.

18 GRAHAM, DON B. "Aesthetic Experience in the Fiction of Frank Norris." University of Texas, 1971.

19 HILL, JOHN S. "Frank Norris's Heroines." University of Wisconsin, 1960.

20 HYDE, FREDERIC G. "American Literature and the Spanish-American War: A Study of the Work of Crane, Norris, Fox, and R. H. Davis." University of Pennsylvania, 1963.

21 JOHNSON, GEORGE W. "Romance and Realism in the Novels of Frank Norris." Columbia University, 1960.

22 KAPLAN, CHARLES. "Frank Norris and the Craft of Fiction." Northwestern University, 1952.

23 KLEIN KARL-HEINZ. "Frank Norris' Erzählungswerk im Verhältnis zu seiner Kunsttheorie." University of Marburg, 1952.

24 LABRIE, RODRIQUE E. "American Naturalism: A View from Within." Pennsylvania State University, 1964.

Doctoral Dissertations

25 LENEHAN, WILLIAM T. "Techniques and Themes in Early English and
American Naturalistic Novels: A Study of the Early Novels of
George Gissing, W. Somerset Maugham, Hamlin Garland, Stephen
Crane, and Frank Norris." University of Oklahoma, 1964.

26 LUNDY, ROBERT D. "The Making of McTeague and The Octopus."
University of California, Berkeley, 1956.

27 MARCHAND, ERNEST L. "Frank Norris: A Study." University of
Wisconsin, 1938.

28 MC ELRATH, JOSEPH R., JR. "A Critical Edition of Frank Norris's
Moran of the Lady Letty: A Story of Adventure Off The California Coast." University of South Carolina, 1973.

29 MITCHELL, MARVIN O. "A Study of Realistic and Romantic Elements
in the Fiction of E. W. Howe, Joseph Kirkland, Hamlin Garland,
Harold Frederic, and Frank Norris (1882-1902)." University
of North Carolina, 1953.

30 OLAFSON, ROBERT B. "Frank Norris' Seven Novels: A Study of the
Mosaic of Tensions Between Critical Realism and Naturalism
in the Works." University of Washington, 1964.

31 PEHOWSKI, MARIAN F. "Darwinism and the Naturalistic Novel:
J. P. Jacobsen, Frank Norris and Shimazaki Tōson." University of Wisconsin, 1973.

32 RAMSAY, ORRINGTON C. "Frank Norris and Environment." University
of Wisconsin, 1950.

33 RAY, JOSEPH R. "Symbolism in the Novels of Frank Norris." University of Texas, 1962.

34 ROBERTS, DEXTER M. "A Psychological Interpretation of Social
Philosophy in the Work of Frank Norris, American Literary
Naturalist." Stanford University, 1967.

35 SCHLOSS, GILBERT A. "Frank Norris: Form and Development."
University of Wisconsin, 1963.

36 SMITH, MARTHA S. "A Study of the Realistic Treatment of Psychic
Phenomena in Selected Fiction of William Dean Howells, Hamlin
Garland, Henry James, Frank Norris, and Theodore Dreiser."
University of North Carolina, 1972.

Doctoral Dissertations

37 WALCUTT, CHARLES C. "Naturalism in the American Novel." University of Michigan, 1938.

38 WALKER, FRANKLIN D. "Frank Norris: A Biographical and Critical Study." University of California, Berkeley, 1932.

WORKS IN FOREIGN LANGUAGES

1   BAECKELMANS, LODE. "Amerikaansche letteren...[Frank Norris],"
    Bibliotheekgids, IV (December 1925), 175-76.

2   BERG, RUBEN G. Moderana Amerikaner. Stockholm: Gebers, 1925,
    pp. 182-84.

3   BIENCOURT, MARIUS. Une Influence du Naturalisme Français en
    Amérique: Frank Norris. Paris: Giard, 1933.

4   BRUNS, FRIEDRICH. Die Amerikanische Dichtung der Gegenwart.
    Berlin and Leipzig: Teubner, 1930, pp. 18-22.

5   FISCHER, WALTHER PAUL. Amerikanische Prosa vom Burgerkrieg bis
    auf die Gegenwart (1863-1922). Leipzig and Berlin: Teubner,
    1926, pp. 57-59.

6   _____. Die englische Literatur de Vereinigten Staaten von
    Nordamerika. Wildpark-Potsdam: Akademische Verlagsgesell-
    schaft Athenaion, [1929], p. 113.

7   HELLSTRÖM, GUSTAF. "'Vilda Vasten': I Nyare Amerikanst Litter-
    atur," Var Tid: Arsbok Utgiven ev Samfundet de Nio, X (1925),
    47-91.

8   JENSEN, JOHANNES V. Die Neue Welt. Berlin, 1908, pp. 109-135.

9   _____. "Frank Norris: The Octopus!," Marz, I (April 1907),
    67-73.

10 KELLNER, LEON. Geschichte der nordamerikanischen Literatur.
    Berlin: Göschen, 1913, I, p. 19; II, p. 89. See 1915.2.

11 KERST, HENRI. "Romanciers américains contemporains" in Cahiers
    des Langues Modernes, I. Paris: Librairie Didier, [1946],
    pp. 31-32, passim.

Works in Foreign Languages

12 KRANENDONK, ANTHONIUS GERARDUS VAN. Geschiedenis van de Ameri-
    kaanse Literatur, I. Amsterdam: G. A. van Oorschot, 1946,
    pp. 310-12.

13 LANZINGER, KLAUS. "Das epische Grundkonzept in Frank Norris's
    Weizentrilogie," Die Neueren Sprachen (1963), 437-51.

14 MICHAUD, REGIS. Panorama de la Litterature Americaine Contemp-
    oraine. Paris: Kra, 1926, pp. 139-41.

15 SALVAN, ALBERT JACQUES. Zola aux Etats-Unis (Brown University
    Studies, 8). Providence: Brown University, 1943, pp. 166-
    74.

16 SAPORTA, MARC. Histoire du Roman Américain. Paris: Seghers,
    1970, pp. 111-13, passim.

17 SCHEFFAUER, HERMAN GEORGE. "Amerikanische Literature der Gegen-
    wart," Deutsche Rundschau, CLXXXVI (February 1921), 215-22.

18 VALERIO, A. "Frank Norris: Sa Vie--Son Oeuvre," Revue de
    l'Enseignement des Langues Vivantes, XXXII (1915), 330-35,
    377-96; XXXIII (1916), 49-62.

Author Index

Each entry carries a reference to year and entry number. Doctoral dissertations are designated with "D" and works in foreign language with "F".

115

AUTHOR INDEX

Chase, Richard V. 1957.1
Childs, James 1964.3
Chislett, William 1928.1
Clark, Harry Hayden 1955.1
Cleaton, Allen 1937.1
Cleaton, Irene 1937.1
Clift, Denison Hailey 1907.1
Cobb, Irvin S. 1928.2
Collins, Carvel 1950.2, 1965.3
Commager, Henry Steele 1950.3
Coolidge, John S. 1957.2
Cooper, Frederic Taber 1899.20,
   1900.4, 1901.5, 1902.5,
   1903.7-8, 1911.1, 1914.1
Cooperman, Stanley 1959.2
Coryn, Sidney G. P. 1909.1
Cottrell, George W. 1930.1
Cowie, Alexander 1948.1
Cowley, Malcolm 1947.3-4,
   1950.4, 1954.2
Crane, Maurice A. 1956.2
Craven, Avery 1947.5
Crisler, Jesse S. D5
Cunliffe, Marcus 1954.3
Curley, Dorothy Nyren 1960.4,
   1969.1
Curti, Merle 1943.1

D. 1899.21
Davenport, Eleanor M. 1897.1
Davidson, Marshall B. 1973.1
Davison, Richard A. 1964.4,
   1966.1, 1968.2-3, 1969.2, D6
Deegan, Dorothy Yost 1951.1
Dell, Floyd 1913.1
De Mille, George E. 1931.4
Dew, Marjorie 1972.2
Dickerson, Lynn C. D7
Dickinson, A. T., Jr. 1971.4
Dickinson, Thomas H. 1932.4
Dillingham, William B. 1960.1,
   1961.1, 1969.3, 1971.5, D8
Dobie, Charles Caldwell 1928.3-
   4, 1931.5-6
Dondore, Dorothy Anne 1926.3

Dreiser, Theodore 1928.5, 1931.7,
   1932.5, 1934.2
Duffus, R. L. 1947.6

East, Harry M. 1912.1
Edgar, Randolph 1909.2, 1916.1,
   1923.1, 1930.2
Edgett, Edwin Francis (E. F. E.)
   1914.5
Edmondson, Elsie F. L. D9
Edwards, Herbert W. 1952.3
Eichelberger, Clayton L. 1971.6
Eldredge, Zoeth Skinner 1915.1
Elias, Robert H. 1959.3
Everett, Wallace W. 1930.3

F. C. B. 1903.18
Fairchild, Hoxie N. 1930.1
Falk, Robert P. 1959.4
Farrell, James T. 1946.1
Figg, Robert M. D10
Fink, Sister Mary J. D11
Firkins, Oscar W. 1924.1
Fischer, Walther Paul F5-6
Fitch, George Hamlin 1899.23,
   1901.8, 1903.19
Flory, Claude Rehard 1969.4
Flower, B. O. 1902.10, 1903.20
Foerster, Norman 1930.4
Folsom, James K. 1962.2
Ford, James L. 1900.5
Francis, H. E. 1959.5
French, John C. 1934.3
French, Warren G. 1962.3, 1967.1
Frohock, W. M. 1969.5
Fullerton, B. M. 1932.6

Gaer, Joseph 1934.4
Gardner, Joseph H. D12
Gardner, Sara J. H. D13
Garland, Hamlin 1903.29, 1931.8
Garnett, Edward 1922.1
Garson, Helen S. D14
Geismar, Maxwell 1947.7, 1953.1,
   1960.2

AUTHOR INDEX

AUTHOR INDEX

Levick, Milne B. 1905.1
Lewis, Oscar 1930.6, 1931.11
Lewisohn, Ludwig 1932.8
Loggin, Vernon 1937.2
Lohf, Kenneth A. 1959.7
London, Jack 1901:13
Lummis, Charles F. 1899.32-33,
    1900.10-11, 1901.14
Lutwack, Leonard 1970.10
Lundy, Robert D. 1957.4, D26
Lynn, Kenneth S. 1955.4, 1958.4
Lyon, Peter 1963.1

M. 1899.34
McCluskey, John E. 1972.6
McCole, C. John 1937.2
McCormick, John 1957.5
McElrath, Joseph R., Jr. D28
McGaffey, Ernest 1901.17
McKee, Irving 1948.3
Mabie, Hamilton W. 1903.35
Mackay, Margaret 1968.6
Malin, Irving 1965.4
Manning, John J. 1968.4
Marble, Annie Russell 1928.9
Marchand, Ernest L. 1942.4, D27
Marcosson, Isaac F. 1898.5,
    1899.35-36, 1901.15, 1903.36,
    1920.1, 1959.8
Markham, Edwin 1914.8, 1931.12
Martin, Jay 1967.4
Martin, Willard E., Jr. 1935.2-3,
    1963.3
Marx, Leo 1959.9, 1964.6
Matthiessen, F. O. 1951.5
May, Henry F. 1964.7
Mencken, Henry Louis 1917.1,
    1926.4, 1928.10
Meyer, George Wilbur 1942.5,
    1943.2
Michaud, Régis F14
Mighels, Ella S. C. 1893.1
Millard, Bailey 1902.17, 1903.37-
    38
Millgate, Michael 1959.10,
    1964.8

Mitchell, Marvin O. D29
Morgan, H. Wayne 1965.5
Morley, Christopher 1928.11
Morley, S. O. 1947.8
Muller, Herbert Joseph 1937.4
Mumford, Lewis 1926.5
Muzzey, A. L. 1902.18

Nilon, Charles H. 1970.11
Noble, David W. 1968.7
Norris, Charles G. 1914.11-12,
    1928.12, 1931.13, 1941.2
Norris, Kathleen 1925.2, 1928.13

O'Connor, William Van 1952.4
O'Dell, Barry 1930.7
Olafson, Robert B. D30
Oracle, K. B. 1891.3
Overton, Grant 1928.14, 1929.4

Paine, Albert Bigelow 1903.44
Pancoast, Henry S. 1918.1
Parrington, Vernon Louis 1928.15,
    1930.8
Pattee, Fred Lewis 1915.3, 1923.
    4, 1930.9
Patteson, Mary L. 1903.45
Payne, William Morton 1903.46
Pehowski, Marian F. D31
Peixotto, Ernest 1933.4
Piper, Henry Dan 1956.3
Pizer, Donald 1955.5, 1958.5,
    1961.5, 1962.9-11, 1963.2,
    1964.9-10, 1965.6, 1966.3-4,
    1970.12
Pochmann, Henry O. 1957.6
Pollock, Channing 1943.3
Preston, Harriet Waters 1903.55

Quinn, Arthur Hobson 1936.4,
    1951.6

Rainsford, W. S. 1903.56
Ramsay, Orrington C. D32
Rankin, T. E. 1922.3

AUTHOR INDEX

Ray, Joseph R.   D33
Redlich, Rosemarie   1952.5
Reniger, H. Willard   1940.2
Rexroth, Kenneth   1964.11
Rice, Wallace   1901.28
Richards, Grant   1934.6
Roberts, Dexter M.   D34

S. '03   1914.17
S. D. S., Jr.   1903.63
Salvan, Albert Jacques   F15
Sanborn, Annie W.   1899.49
Sanchez, Nellie Van de Grift
    1904.1, 1920.2
Saporta, Marc   F16
Scheffauer, Herman George   F17
Scherman, David E.   1952.5
Schloss, Gilbert A.   D35
Schneider, Robert W.   1962.12,
    1965.7
Sheehy, Eugene P.   1959.7
Sherwood, John R.   1958.6
Shinn, Charles Howard   1899.57
Simonds, William E.   1909.8
Sinclair, Upton   1925.3
Slosson, Edwin E.   1910.1,
    1915.4
Smith, Bernard   1939.2
Smith, Dorothy J.   1972.7
Smith, Guy E.   1957.7
Smith, Martha S.   D36
Snell, George   1947.9
Spangler, George M.   1973.6
Spiller, Robert E.   1948.4-5,
    1955.6, 1958.7
Stanton, Theodore   1909.10
Stephens, Henry Morse   1903.65,
    1914.18
Stone, Edward   1966.5
Stovall, Floyd   1943.4
Straumann, Heinrich   1965.8
Strong, Austin   1944.2
Stronks, James B.   1970.13,
    1971.8
Swanberg, W. A.   1965.9
Swensson, John K.   1971.9

Taylor, Gordon O.   1969.8
Taylor, Harvey   1930.10
Taylor, Walter Fuller   1936.5,
    1937.5, 1942.6
Tebbel, John   1948.6
Thompson, Francis   1903.70
Thorp, Willard   1960.5
Todd, Edgeley W.   1959.11
Todd, Frank M.   1902.21
Tompkins, Juliet Wilbor   1928.16
Trent, William Peterfield   1921.1

Underwood, John Curtis   1914.20

Valerio, A   F18
Van Doren, Carl   1925.4, 1929.5,
    1940.3
Van Doren, Mark   1925.4
Van Westrum, A. Schade   1899.61,
    1901.31, 1903.72
Vance, William L.   1970.14

Wagenknecht, Edward C.   1930.11,
    1952.6
Wager, Willis   1968.8
Walcutt, Charles C.   1941.3, 1947.
    10, 1948.7, 1956.4, 1962.13,
    D37
Walker, Don D.   1967.5
Walker, Franklin D.   1931.14,
    1932.10, 1935.4, 1956.5,
    1960.6, 1966.6, 1967.6,
    1970.15, D37
Walker, Philip   1967.7
Ward, Alfred C.   1932.9
Watson, Charles S.   1972.8
Weinberg, Herman G.   1972.9
West, Ray B., Jr.   1952.7
Wheeler, Otis B.   1970.16
White, William   1959.12
Williams, Harold H.   1918.2
Wilson, Edmund   1950.7
Wister, Owen   1903.73
Witham, W. Tasker   1947.11
Wood, William Allen   1902.23
Woodress, James   1968.9

AUTHOR INDEX

Selected Subject and Title Index

The symbol † indicates a review of the work cited.

After Strange Gods 1928.12

The American Public and "Popular" Fiction 1973.4

An American School of Fiction 1964.8

Bandy Callaghan's Girl 1931.3†, 11

A Bargain with Peg-leg 1903.9†, 69†.

SELECTED SUBJECT AND TITLE INDEX

SELECTED SUBJECT AND TITLE INDEX

A Defense of the Flag 1902.12

The Dis-Associated Charities F18

The Dual Personality of Slick Dick Nickerson 1905.1

Dying Fires 1909.15†; 1930.9, 11; 1952.1; 1953.1;
    1954.6; 1956.5; 1962.7; 1966.7

The End of the Act 1928.12, F18

The End of the Beginning 1931.3†; 1958.6

Les Enerves de Jumieges 1931.14

The Exile's Toast 1907.2; 1916.1; 1926.2; 1930.4;
    1956.5

Fantaisie Printanière 1931.2†-3†, 9†, 11; 1932.3;
    1936.4; 1955.4

Fiction Writing as a Business 1928.14

The Finding of Lieutenant Outhwaite 1931.14

Frank Norris of "The Wave" 1931.2†-3†, 9†; 1934.1;
    1940.1

Frank Norris' Weekly Letter (25 May 1901) 1968.2

Frank Norris' Weekly Letter (1 June 1901) 1968.2

Frank Norris' Weekly Letter (8 June 1901) 1966.1

Frank Norris' Weekly Letter (15 June 1901) 1968.2

Frank Norris' Weekly Letter (29 June 1901 1966.1;
    1968.2

Frank Norris' Weekly Letter (6 July 1901) 1968.2

Frank Norris' Weekly Letter (13 July 1901) 1964.4

Frank Norris' Weekly Letter (20 July 1901) 1970.13

Frank Norris' Weekly Letter (3 August 1901) 1962.10;
    1964.4; 1967.7

SELECTED SUBJECT AND TITLE INDEX

Frank Norris' Weekly Letter (10 August 1901)   1968.2

Frank Norris' Weekly Letter (24 August 1901)   1966.4

Frank Norris' Weekly Letter (31 August 1901)   1968.2

Gaston le Fox 1934.5; 1941.1; 1942.6; 1967.2

The Ghost in the Cross-Trees 1903.69†

The "Great American Novelist 1965.1; 1973.4

The Great Corner in Hannibal and St. Jo 1971.9

The Great Szarrattar Opal 1931.14

Grettir at Drangey 1930.11; 1947.8

Grettir at Thornhall-Stead 1930.3

The Guest of Honor 1909.17†; 1930.11; F18

Happiness by Conquest 1973.5

The Herosim of Jonesee 1928.12; 1941.1

His Dead Mother's Portrait 1928.12

His Single Blessedness 1928.12; 1962.4

His Sister 1936.4; 1953.3

The House with the Blinds 1903.6; 1909.4†, 15†;
   1953.3; F18

In Defense of Doctor W. Lawlor 1902.12; 1905.1;
   1932.10; 1943.3

In the Heat of Battle 1965.7

In the Veldt of the Transvaal 1947.1

An Industrial Renaissance in Japan 1973.5

Inside an Organ 1931.11

It Was a Close Call 1973.4

SELECTED SUBJECT AND TITLE INDEX

SELECTED SUBJECT AND TITLE INDEX

Moving a Fifty-Ton Gun <u>1931</u>.11

Mr. Kipling's Kim <u>1973</u>.5

The National Spirit as It Relates to the "Great American
    Novel" <u>1936</u>.3

The "Nature" Revival in Literature <u>1965</u>.1; <u>1973</u>.4

The Navy of Japan <u>1973</u>.5

The Need of a Literary Conscience <u>1933</u>.4

A Neglected Epic <u>1902</u>.11; <u>1903</u>.39†, 59†; <u>1956</u>.5;
    <u>1959</u>.11

New Year's at San Quentin <u>1965</u>.7

New York as a Literary Centre <u>1928</u>.14; <u>1966</u>.4; <u>1973</u>.4

News Gathering at Key West <u>1932</u>.10; <u>1956</u>.5

Newspaper Criticisms and American Fiction <u>1928</u>.14;
    <u>1973</u>.4

The Novel with a "Purpose" <u>1903</u>.70†; <u>1911</u>.1; <u>1928</u>.14;
    <u>1936</u>.4; <u>1943</u>.2; <u>1951</u>.6; <u>1956</u>.4; <u>1960</u>.3; 1962.3;
    <u>1964</u>.2, 4; <u>1965</u>.1

Novelists of the Future <u>1905</u>.2; <u>1928</u>.14; <u>1964</u>.8

Novelists to Order--While You Wait <u>1905</u>.1; <u>1973</u>.4

<u>The Octopus</u> <u>1899</u>.29; <u>1900</u>.9; <u>1901</u>.1†-12†, 14†-15†, 16,
    18†-33†; <u>1902</u>.3†-4†, 5-7, 10†, 14, 16-18†, 19†, 22-
    24; <u>1903</u>.3-4, 14, 16-21, 23, 25, 27-29, 32-33, 36,
    38, 43-49, 52, 54-55†, 64-65, 68, 72-73; <u>1905</u>.1-2;
    <u>1909</u>.8, 10, 12, 14; <u>1911</u>.1; <u>1912</u>.1-2; <u>1913</u>.1; <u>1914</u>.4,
    8, 10, 20, 24-25; <u>1915</u>.1, 3; <u>1918</u>.2; <u>1919</u>.1; <u>1920</u>.1;
    <u>1922</u>.1-3; <u>1923</u>.2; <u>1925</u>.1, 3-4; <u>1926</u>.1, 5-6; <u>1927</u>.1-2;
    <u>1928</u>.2-4, 15; <u>1929</u>.2-5; <u>1930</u>.1-3, 6-9, 11; <u>1931</u>.1,
    3, 9-12, 14; <u>1932</u>.1-4, 7, 10; <u>1933</u>.1-2, 4; <u>1934</u>.1,
    3, 5; <u>1935</u>.1-3; <u>1936</u>.4; <u>1937</u>.1, 3-4; <u>1939</u>.1; <u>1940</u>.1-
    3; <u>1941</u>.1-2; <u>1942</u>.1, 3, 6; <u>1943</u>.1-2, 4; <u>1944</u>.1;
    <u>1946</u>.1; <u>1947</u>.1, 3-6†, 8-10; <u>1948</u>.1, 3-4, 6; <u>1950</u>.3-
    5; <u>1951</u>.3, 6; <u>1952</u>.1, 3, 6; <u>1953</u>.1; <u>1954</u>.1, 3, 5-6;
    <u>1955</u>.1-6; <u>1956</u>.4-5; <u>1957</u>.1, 4, 7; <u>1958</u>.1-5; <u>1959</u>.1,
    5, 8-9, 11; <u>1960</u>.1, 5; <u>1961</u>.3; <u>1962</u>.2-3, 6-10, 12;
    <u>1963</u>.2; <u>1964</u>.1-2, 4-6, 8; <u>1965</u>.1-3, 5, 7-8; <u>1966</u>.3,
    7; <u>1967</u>.2, 4-5, 7; <u>1968</u>.3, 5, 7; <u>1969</u>.2, 4-5; <u>1970</u>.4,
    9, 14, 16; <u>1971</u>.2-4, 10; <u>1972</u>.2, 7; <u>1973</u>.1-3, F14-15;
    F18

SELECTED SUBJECT AND TITLE INDEX

SELECTED SUBJECT AND TITLE INDEX

Retail Bookseller: Literary Dictator 1928.14

A Reversion to Type 1903.6; 1909.12†; 1923.3; 1958.2;
    1961.5; 1965.7; 1967.2; 1970.6; F15

The Rickshaw that Happened 1970.13

The Riding of Felipe 1903.69†; 1930.11; 1962.3; F18

Robert d' Artois 1907.1; 1914.9; 1928.3, 4, 12;
    1957.2; 1965.7; F18

Salt and Sincerity 1902.13, 28; 1911.1; 1912.2;
    1923.4; 1951.4; 1956.5; 1964.8

A Salvation Boom in Matabeleland 1928.12; 1941.1;
    1965.7

Shanghaied See also Moran of the Lady Letty 1899.22†,
    25†, 37, 45†-46, 50†-56†; 1900.12, 15, 28, 30†;
    1934.6; 1956.5

The Ship That Saw a Ghost 1903.69†; 1905.1; 1953.1;
    1967.5; F18

Shorty Stack, Pugilist 1909.14†; 1930.9

The Son of the Sheik 1902.12; 1928.3-4; 1930.3;
    1931.14; 1940.1; 1947.1; 1958.2; 1965.7; 1967.2;
    1970.6; 1973.5

A South-Sea Expedition 1931.11

The Spinners' Book of Fiction 1908.1†

A Statue in an Old Garden 1907.1

Story-Tellers vs. Novelists 1912.1; 1928.14; 1970.13

A Strange Relief-Ship 1973.5

The Strangest Thing F18

Student Life in Paris 1956.5; 1969.3

Suggestions 1928.12; 1947.1; 1965.7

SELECTED SUBJECT AND TITLE INDEX

The Surrender of Santiago 1928.12; 1932.10; 1953.1;
    1956.5; 1966.7

The Third Circle 1897.1; 1903.6; 1909.4†-5, 9†, 12†,
    14†-15†, 17†; 1914.20; 1928.8, 12; 1930.3, 9, 11;
    1931.12; 1936.1; 1953.1

The Third Circle 1909.1†-4†, 6†- 7.†, 9†, 11†, 12†-
    17†; 1923.3; 1931.2; 1932.10; 1934.1; 1940.1;
    1952.1; 1953.1; 1962.3; 1965.7; 1973.5; F18

"This Animal of a Buldy Jones" 1899.6, 20; 1902.17;
    1909.9†; 1941.1

Thoroughbred 1941.1; 1965.7

To the Erie 1956.5

Told by Frank Norris 1973.4

Toppan 1909.9†, 12†; 1930.11; 1958.2

Travis Hallett's Half Back 1931.14; 1965.7; 1966.7

The True Reward of the Novelist 1903.70†; 1905.2;
    1911.1; 1912.1; 1928.14; F18

Two Hearts That Beat as One 1902.21; 1915.4; 1973.5;
    F18

Two Pair 1902.21; 1903.4; 1930.3; 1931.14

Unequally Yoked 1931.11, 14

The Unknown Author and the Publisher 1973.5

Vandover and the Brute 1914.1†-6†, 8-10†, 11-12,
    13†-16†, 18†-20, 21†-26†; 1915.2-3; 1917.2;
    1918.1; 1919.1; 1928.3-4, 10, 12, 15; 1929.2-3;
    1930.3, 8, 11; 1931.9, 14; 1932.7, 10; 1933.2;
    1934.1, 3, 5; 1936.4; 1937.1-2; 1940.1; 1941.1;
    1942.6; 1944.1; 1947.1, 4-5, 8, 10; 1948.4, 7;
    1950.3-5; 1951.1, 6; 1952.1, 3, 6; 1953.1; 1954.6;
    1955.1-2, 4; 1956.3-5; 1957.1-7; 1959.1-2, 5;
    1960.1, 5; 1961.3, 5; 1962.3, 6, 12-13; 1964.5;
    1965.4-5, 7; 1966.3, 7; 1967.2-3, 5; 1968.1, 5,
    7-8; 1969.3, 5; 1970.3, 12, 16; 1971.7, 10; F14;
    F18

SELECTED SUBJECT AND TITLE INDEX